SAFFRON HOWDEN is a mum, journalist and national leader in media literacy. She co-founded and edited Australia's only national newspaper for kids, *Crinkling News*, and pioneered children's news literacy programs. She has worked for major news organisations, including *The Sydney Morning Herald*, *The Daily Telegraph* and AAP. She was Google News Initiative's first Teaching Fellow for Australia & New Zealand and worked with Facebook Asia Pacific to produce a digital citizenship curriculum for the region.

DHANA QUINN is a freelance writer and mother of three. She has worked as a radio, television and print journalist for *The Age*, *Crinkling News* and the ABC. She was also a presenter on the ABC's education program *Behind the News*. She holds a Master of International and Community Development and has qualifications in editing and English language teaching.

'Saffron Howden is a ceaseless campaigner for making news and media accessible to kids. It's such important work. *Kid Reporter* is the perfect gift for the curious, smart young person in your life.'

Annabel Crabb, journalist, TV presenter and political writer

'Clear, simple, direct and engaging, *Kid Reporter* isn't just for kids. If you want to be a journalist, if you care about the news or you're a journalist who wants to remind yourself about how the job is done, this book is for you. It is a wonderful, timely guide to what news is, how it's produced and why it matters. After more than 30 years in the game, even I learned a thing or two.'

Peter Greste, Professor of Journalism, University of Queensland

'Saffron Howden and Dhana Quinn let everyone in on the secret all newshounds understand: being a reporter is so much fun! It is also challenging and fascinating – a craft that can be learned and mastered. In *Kid Reporter*, they use their great experience as journalists and editors to explain how reporting happens and how you go about finding and telling great stories. For the student who already loves stories of all kinds, and for parents and teachers who want to encourage curiosity, creativity and skills for life-long learning: *Kid Reporter* is a wonderful book.'

Mark Scott AO, Secretary, NSW Department of Education

'A great guide to what journalists do, how they do it and why it matters. Worth reading for young and old.'

Margaret Simons, freelance journalist and Honorary Principal Fellow, Centre for Advancing Journalism, University of Melbourne

KID REPORTER

The Secret to

BREAKING NEWS

SAFFRON HOWDEN & DHANA QUINN

NEWSOUTH

A NewSouth book

Published by
NewSouth Publishing
University of New South Wales Press Ltd
University of New South Wales
Sydney NSW 2052
AUSTRALIA
newsouthpublishing.com

ISBN   9781742237145 (paperback)
           9781742245164 (ebook)
           9781742249728 (ePDF)

 A catalogue record for this book is available from the National Library of Australia

Design Josephine Pajor-Markus
Cover design Design by Committee
Internal images Adobe Stock, Dreamstime, Shutterstock, VectorStock

All reasonable efforts were taken to obtain permission to use copyright material reproduced in this book, but in some cases copyright could not be traced. The authors welcome information in this regard.

To Amelie, Asha, Charlie, Peta

and

all the kids who loved and read *Crinkling News*

CONTENTS

PART IV: GET READY TO PUBLISH

INTRODUCTION

If you are reading this book, there's a good chance you'd like to become a journalist. Or maybe you want to start a school newspaper. Or learn about where news comes from and how it's put together. Perhaps you dream of standing in front of a TV camera and interviewing famous people. Or reporting on big, breaking news.

The job of a reporter is very important. It's a big responsibility. But it's also a lot of fun!

Journalists find out what's going on before nearly everybody else. They are on the ground when major events happen. They investigate and ask tough questions of powerful people.

Their stories can change lives and make the world a better place. By bringing news to their communities, reporters keep us all informed and connected.

But this book is useful for any young Australian – not just budding journalists. Whether you're interested in current affairs, sport, the arts or technology, there's something in these pages for you. Aspiring photographers, illustrators, designers, video producers and editors will also find it helpful.

Anyone who wants to learn more about the media – or who loves writing, researching, uncovering secrets and investigating – will find plenty of handy tricks and tips.

Not only that, we'll show you how to turn your curiosity into a front-page scoop!

For too long news has been for adults only. But what happens in the world affects you too. We think it's about time young people were more involved in making the news. *Kid Reporter* will help you find and use your voice.

Step-by-step reporter's guide

Sharing news comes naturally to most humans. We're all interested in what's happening around us. And when we discover new information, we want to tell other people.

This book shows you how to turn natural curiosity into essential journalism skills, like critical thinking, news detecting, interviewing, fact-checking, publishing and broadcasting. We'll guide you through the steps to researching and writing a great news story and producing your own newspaper, podcast or TV-style news program.

Plus, we feature plenty of young reporters – some as young as nine – to inspire you with their journalism journey.

News, media and information

News and media are a big part of modern life. Information comes at us from the television, radio, tablets and smartphones. It's in newspapers and books, online and on social media. Not only an excellent how-to guide, *Kid Reporter* is also your own personal media navigator. After you've read this book, you'll find it easier to sift through all those daily messages bombarding you from dawn until your head hits the pillow at night.

Understanding and identifying your point of view, as well as other people's perspectives and opinions, is another important part of navigating the media. You'll also need to know what questions to ask and find clues to help you decide if information is reliable and accurate, or wrong and misleading. We cover it all here!

Becoming a reporter

One of the best ways to learn about the media is to become a media creator yourself. If you know how to find accurate information for your own news story, you are far more likely to know if another person's work is based on facts.

This book gives you those tools and shows you how to use them in real life. There's almost no chance you'll be fooled by 'fake news' again.

Kid Reporter will give you the confidence to ask questions, speak up and take part.

Your stories matter. And we want to hear them.

HOW TO USE THIS BOOK

Kid Reporter is divided into four parts. In Part I, we start with the fundamentals: what the job of a journalist involves; their role in history, the community and society; and, the basic building blocks of a news story.

Part II describes how to put a story together, including the essential questions that any story needs to answer. We talk about where to get information and how to interview people. We detail the tools required for print and broadcast journalists and provide a guide to photographing and recording. We cover the main positions in a newsroom and how they bring a paper or program to life.

In Part III we do a deep dive into critical thinking and news detection. We walk through perspective, opinion, balance, fact-checking – and how to spot 'fake news'. We tackle ethics and look at the rules that guide professional journalists and news outlets.

Finally, in Part IV, we present a step-by-step guide to setting up a newspaper, podcast and TV-style news program in a school environment. We also showcase the publications and programs of young people who've already embarked on the journalism adventure and ask them how they overcame challenges along the way.

Throughout the book there are plenty of activities and examples for you to practise your newfound reporting skills – with friends, classmates, or on your own.

Ask adults for help

While it might sound like fun to be an independent young journalist working alone, producing news is hard work. It can sometimes be a bit overwhelming. And it costs money. Somebody has to pay for the paper, printing, camera, computer, even the notepad and pen!

Getting at least one trusted adult on board before you start your first real news story is essential. This could be a parent or teacher, for example. An adult can help you get the permission you need to interview someone, find a contact phone number or email address if you can't, or organise access to a computer or editing software. They might also be able to investigate how your stories will be published or have ideas about how to raise money if you need it.

Your safety and wellbeing must come first. Never interview a stranger without adult supervision. And don't take photographs or record people without their permission. We cover these issues in the book, but you will still need a trusted adult by your side to answer questions and guide you on your path to becoming a young reporter.

Covering some news can make you sad or worried and talking about it with people who understand, including adults, is vital.

Don't be afraid to ask for help. The more support you have, the more fun you'll have – and the better your chances of achieving what you set out to do.

Welcome to the *Kid Reporter* newsroom. Now, let's get started!

PART I

WHAT DOES A REPORTER DO?

1

THE BASICS

As you're walking home from school one day, you stop to drain the last drops from your battered water bottle when you hear a faint tapping noise coming from above.

You look up and see a possum in a tree. But this little brushtail has a large glass jar stuck on its head! It is trying to get the glass off by repeatedly hitting the jar against the tree trunk.

What would you do in this situation?

1   Think it's a bit weird but keep walking?
2   Find a trusted adult, explain what you've seen, and hope that person will call for help?
3   Find a trusted adult and ask them to call a wildlife rescue group or the local emergency services? Then – if you can – stick around to see what happens next? All the while your mind is ticking over with so many questions: 'How does a possum get a jar on its head?', 'Who will come to the rescue?', 'Has this ever happened before?' Most importantly, 'Will the possum be okay?' Then you think to yourself, 'I can't wait to tell my friends about this.'

NEWS | POLICE

Possum needed a little police magic

BY B.C LEWIS

A HIGH level emergency services operation was needed to rescue a possum on June 11 who was stuck up a tree in Blaxland with a glass jar on his head.

Blue Mountains Police Rescue found the possum with the tomato paste jar stuck over its head between 15 and 20 metres up a tree in Winncoopa Road. It's believed the jar had been stuck on its head for at least eight or nine hours.

A Parramatta Fire and Rescue NSW crew brought in its elevated hydraulic platform. Police Rescue grabbed the possum from the tree, handing it over to a WIRES team who took it to a vet.

Police rescue officer Snr Constable Steve Day said: "We were called out by a local resident ... the possum was banging its head against

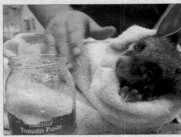

FREE AT LAST: The brushtail possum gets some relief at the Nepean Animal Hospital in Regentville.

a tree with a glass jar on its head.

"The tree was eaten out by white ants so we were unable to get access to it. We called fire and rescue and the Parramatta brigade sent their platform unit up to us.

"We managed to get access to it ... WIRES are taking the possum to the vet ...it's alive, hopefully it will be in good form."

The possum was treated at Nepean Animal Hospital in Regentville later that afternoon. Vet nurse Tegan Borg said the possum was distressed on arrival but he was weighed, sedated and once they put lubricant on the whole jar, "we angled it differently and it came off quite easily".

"It was a pasta sauce jar and was pretty clean, he had given it a good lick," Ms Borg said.

"He was lucky he could still breathe. He was stuck by the jaw, his neck is a tiny bit swollen, we've given him some pain relief and fluid. He doesn't seem too badly injured. He'll probably go back with the WIRES carer today once he's fully awake."

Ms Borg said they treated all wildlife and strays for free. She encouraged residents to contain rubbish and wash jars, so possums are "not enticed by smells".

Homeowner Susan Gould said her dog had alerted her to the distressed possum.

The story of a Blue Mountains possum with a glass jar on its head made news across Australia.

Blue Mountains Gazette and Australian Community Media

If you chose (3) you are undoubtedly a curious person. And a reporter needs to be inquisitive. Journalists are like detectives; they want to get the full story – the who, what, when, where, why and how.

Amazingly, a possum really did get a jar stuck on its head. We are not making it up! It happened one winter day on a suburban street in the Blue Mountains west of

Sydney in New South Wales. The story was covered by the local newspaper, the *Blue Mountains Gazette*. It even made it to the national television news as well as news websites across the country.

People were interested partly because of the large number of people involved. Police, a fire and rescue crew, wildlife rescuers and vets worked together to reach the possum, carefully get it down from the tree, and safely remove the jar.

Luckily, the story had a happy ending. The male brushtail was released back onto the same tree the next night – minus the glass jar.

What is a journalist?

A journalist is a person who finds out what's happening in the community and around the world. They then tell an audience about it through the media. That might be on radio, television, or in newspapers, magazines, videos, podcasts and news websites. Journalists don't spread rumours or gossip. They carefully gather new information and facts. Reporters keep the public informed by presenting that information in a balanced and interesting way.

Their job is very important because it keeps an eye on what powerful people and organisations are doing. They let the rest of us know when somebody breaks the rules or harms others. News stories are non-fiction.

A journalist:
- researches
- investigates
- interviews
- gathers and checks facts
- writes or presents information
- tells a true story.

Journalists are sometimes called reporters or correspondents.

To become a reporter, you will need to find out what is really going on around you. Speaking to experts and eye-witnesses, researching and gathering evidence is essential to get to the truth. Only then can you share that knowledge with others.

Meet a real-life young reporter: Matisse Veerman

Matisse started *Hot Chips News* because she loved writing and wanted to find other students who did, too. 'I had also entered a newspaper competition and came third, and that inspired me to start up my own newspaper,' she said.

In Year 5 at Camp Hill State Infants and Primary School in Queensland, Matisse found some supportive teachers to get the project off the ground. 'They helped me find other kids who were interested and helped me with the printing and collating of the paper. My mum also helped me with the layout and to find sponsors for each paper to pay for the printing.'

Matisse was chief editor and 15 students eventually got involved. Each edition focused on a specific topic, such as space and science, water and recycling, animals, and the arts.

'Kids could then choose to research the topic or interview someone in the related field,' Matisse said. 'We also did book reviews and author interviews.

FOR THE KIDS

BY THE KIDS

HOT CHIPS NEWS

ISSUE NO. 4

CAMP HILL STATE INFANTS AND PRIMARY SCHOOL

Welcome!

Hi everyone,
Welcome to the fourth issue of Hot Chips News!
This issue we are talking about community and why we love ours! Thanks for being a part of the Hot Chips community!

Matisse

Art work by Samuel Keane yr4

Art work by Kaitlin McDougall yr4

Art work by Sophie Graham yr6

WELCOME TO THE
GOLD COAST
HOME OF THE
XI COMMONWEALTH GAMES

Check out more fab Games pics on page 8

The Stilers

The Mantiels at the Games

HUMANS OF CAMP HILL

LEANNE MCNAUGHT

Leanne is our fabulous Crossing Supervisor and she lives in Carina. She loves that it feels like we live in a little community even though we are in a big city. Leanne especially loves the children in our community because they become a part of her life. She thinks our community would be improved with less traffic. Leanne is proud that she keeps our children and families safe. Leanne is also a proud volunteer in our community. In her spare time Leanne likes going to markets, swimming in the bay and Clem Jones, visiting Southbank, being in nature and going to Wynnum, especially when it's raining. She also visits friends and goes to Church.

by Wilson Veerman yr3

MR HUNT

Mr Hunt is a year 4 teacher and he lives in Lota. He loves living in our community because it is made of all sorts of people and they all try and get along together. If he could change anything he would like it if people used cars less and used more public transport. Mr Hunt is proud that he can help children appreciate our beautiful environment. With his time off he likes gardening and birdwatching.

by Bavitha Gummadi yr6

SARAH JANE WALSH

Sarah Jane from the Camp Hill Antique Centre loves that we live in a relaxed, friendly environment. "It's a little city that loves to think big. Everyone supports everyone from schools to business' to fundraisers". Sarah Jane wouldn't change anything about Camp Hill. She thinks it's perfect!!! When Sarah Jane and her partner Paul moved their business from Woolloongabba to Camp Hill they were overwhelmed by the local community and the way they were welcomed with open arms.

Sarah Jane is from Tamworth, NSW and loves to do anything with her children that involves the outdoors, sand and water and she believes Brisbane has plenty of these activities.

by Matisse Veerman yr6

1

Kids could create art around the theme or puzzles and word searches, and even a joke column. It was pretty cool seeing what they came up with.'

Over two years Matisse and the newspaper club published eight issues of *Hot Chips News*. Some editions ran over 14 pages.

The paper stopped when Matisse went to high school, but the memories and a public record of the students' work remain.

LEFT The title *Hot Chips News* was inspired by the school's name. 'Chips' is an acronym of **C**amp **H**ill State **I**nfants and **P**rimary **S**chool and 'Hot' is for 'hot off the press'.

Highlights and challenges from Matisse

- 'I liked being able to collaborate with other students and hear their ideas of what to put in the newspaper.'
- 'I learnt different ways of thinking and approaching things.'
- 'It was amazing to see the different abilities of my friends.'
- 'Best of all was hanging out with friends at lunchtime and making something together.'
- 'The most challenging things were getting people to join the newspaper club and to submit their work on time.'

2

A JOURNALIST'S TOOLKIT

Toolkit: Research and investigation

As you would know, whenever you do a school assignment you often have to gather information and facts about an event or issue. Journalists do the same when they cover a news story. They interview people and observe events, actions and details. They also research a topic using books, reports, websites and other sources of knowledge.

There are different types of stories: *news reports* include plenty of facts, dates, places and names; *investigations* involve examining lots of evidence and uncovering hidden information; *features* explore issues or events in more depth; *analyses* pull together all the different strands of a big news story and reach a conclusion; and, *reviews* take a critical look at a book, performance, restaurant, game or movie.

What you need:

access to the internet

access to school or local library

help from a trusted adult

The investigation begins

Let's think about how a reporter might cover an event – something that has just happened.

- Event
  A news event might be an emergency like a bushfire or flood, an election, the Olympic Games, the opening of a new sports field, even a prison escape. A journalist needs to find out as much as possible about what has happened so they can accurately report the story.

• Context

It's important to remember there is usually some background to the story that helps make more sense of what has occurred.

For example, a school could be closing in Perth, Western Australia. As a reporter you have to tell your audience what has happened. You will need the *name* of the school, the name of the suburb in which it's located, the *number* of students and teachers, *when* the community was told and *when* the school is expected to shut. Then you should help people understand *why* the school is closing and how that is going to affect the students, their families and staff.

Below are examples of what to consider to give context.

» Have student numbers fallen in the past 1, 5 or 10 years?
» Have any other schools closed in the area?
» Has a new school opened nearby?
» Are there fewer children living in the area?

Toolkit: Interviews

What you need:

pen and paper

recording device

help from a
trusted adult

optional
– a telephone

A journalist isn't an expert. Reporters need to speak to different people so they can put together a news story. In order to gather facts, they interview eyewitnesses, experts, those in charge and those involved.

Let's go back to our poor possum on pages 3–5 and add some details. As you read these paragraphs, have a think about who you might interview to tell this news story.

After the possum with a jar on its head was discovered up the tree, Blue Mountains Police Rescue was called. An officer noticed the tree was too dangerous to climb because it had been eaten out by white ants or termites. A hydraulic lift – a machine to lift a rescue worker to reach the possum – was needed.

Luckily the Fire and Rescue NSW crew at Parramatta, a suburb of Sydney, had the equipment. This was turning into quite an operation! Once the team arrived a rescue worker brought the animal down and wildlife carers took it to Nepean Animal Hospital. Phew.

After all that, who would you interview for your news story?

Who to interview

* Eyewitnesses
  People at the scene can tell you what they saw and heard with their own eyes and ears. In the case of the possum, that might be someone who stopped to watch the rescue while walking down the street, or nearby residents who saw events unfold from their front yard. Bystanders are important because they help your audience understand what it felt like to be there.

- People in charge
  Senior police, fire and rescue crew and animal
  care workers managing the rescue can give factual
  information about when the operation started, the
  number of people involved, how it was carried out,
  and details about the outcome. Authorities have
  to keep track of their staff and equipment, so they
  need to carefully record what has happened and
  can share that knowledge with you.

- Experts
  People who have special training or skills in a subject
  can give you history and context for your story.
  For example, you could interview someone from a
  wildlife group or a vet to find out if possums have
  been injured or trapped by rubbish in the past. You
  could speak to someone who studies possums, or
  native Australian marsupials, about the challenges
  faced when humans live near wildlife.

You might also do some research – either by reading
books or seeking information on the internet – on possums to find out about their lives and habitat.

Toolkit: Checking facts

Check the facts – and then re-check the facts. Attention
to detail is extremely important when you're a reporter.

What you need:

- access to the internet
- access to school or local library
- help from a trusted adult

As a journalist you are presenting facts so you need to be very careful that you don't sneak in an extra letter in the spelling of someone's name, or add a few zeros to a number. Your audience is relying on you to get it right.

Can you spot the differences between these two sentences?

Sam Samstone, aged 13, said he found $10.

Sam Sameton, aged 23, said she found $100.

That's right. In the first sentence Sam has a different surname and age, is male not female, and only found $10 – not 10 times that!

A few mistakes or the wrong spelling can mean you are talking about a different person. And the difference between $10 and $100 is large. If you are not sure you could ask Sam to write his or her name down. You might also ask Sam to show you the money – if it hasn't already been spent! – and point out where they found it. Checking with someone who actually saw Sam find the cash is another idea.

- Judgement call
  Journalists need to make good judgements about where and from whom they get information. If you are a reporter covering the school fair, you will want to find out how many people went.

  A friend from class or a person operating one of the rides would be guessing the numbers. But someone running the event can tell you exactly how many tickets were sold and would be the best person to ask. This might be the school principal, or a teacher in charge of the fair.

- Evidence
  You should find evidence to back up a claim, such as a photograph, video or official report. You could also talk to those involved to help build a picture of what occurred. If lots of people who don't know one another tell you the same thing, that's multiple sources making the same claim and is much more likely to be true.

As a journalist, your audience is trusting you to accurately report back on the event.

Toolkit: Writing or presenting

What you need:

- pen/pencil
- computer
- camera or recording device
- platform to publish
- dictionary
- help from a trusted adult

After a reporter has gathered all the information they can through research and interviews, the real fun begins! Journalists then need to put it all together and create a news story. We will talk more about this process in Part II, pages 88–100.

For now, let's think about how to present all those facts in a clear and interesting way for your audience.

When you read a book or story, think about what kind of first sentence makes you want to keep reading. The first sentence is all-important because if it's too complicated or boring people might not bother with the rest of the story. You want it to grab their attention because your story is important.

Which sentence below would make you want to find out more about this event?

There is a hole in a road in the city.

A sinkhole in a city road uncovers a secret tunnel leading to a local bank.

The first sentence is factual. But it's a lot more interesting to discover a sinkhole caused by a secret tunnel that might lead to lots of money in a bank! The extra bit of information at the beginning of the story helps fire

Lead

Did you know that the first sentence of a news story is often called a 'lead'? In journalism, this means the opening sentence or paragraph of your story. It's meant to grab your audience's attention and summarise the key points.

up your audience's imagination. Everybody will want to know more.

Below are some examples of leads, the first sentences of articles written to make the reader want to keep reading.

Lead sentence

'Scientists have found something incredible trapped inside a 98-million-year-old piece of amber: an ancient "hell ant" with blade-like teeth and a metal horn growing out of its forehead.'

Sole survivors
Mystery and magic in these old shoes

BY Dhana Quinn

IF YOU LIVE in an old house, there just might be a little bit of magic hiding in the walls.

People around the world have been finding shoes in walls, under floorboards, in chimneys and in roofs. Recently a boot was found behind a fireplace in an old children's law court in Sydney.

Hidden shoes are mysterious because no one knows for sure why they were put there.

But some people believe they were a lucky charm and part of folk magic from a long time ago.

IT'S A MYSTERY

Dr Ian Evans is an Australian historian and he stumbled upon this mystery a few years ago. He says when people renovate or knock down homes they often find things and don't think much of it.

Some objects make their way into weird places by chance, such as a coin falling through a crack in the floor.

"[But] there are many objects that cannot be explained as the result of accidental loss or the actions of children or animals," he says.

There's lots of evidence that some shoes were deliberately hidden.

WITCHES AND DEMONS

It's hard to imagine what it might have been like to

live in Australia 100 years ago. Or in England 400 years ago.

Dr Evans says we know a lot more about science and medicine today, but the past was a very different place and people could be superstitious.

They believed in witches, demons and evil spirits and they were really scared of them.

"This was a time when illness was often thought to be the result of spells cast by an enemy or the work of evil beings," he says.

"There wasn't a local doctor, like we have today, who

could diagnose what was wrong and prescribe medicine.

"So to deal with this fear and to protect themselves from 'bad' things, they used folk magic and lucky charms."

BUT WHY A SHOE?

Rebecca Shawcross looks after one of the largest shoe collections in the world at Northampton Museums and Art Gallery in England. She says no one really knows when and how this habit began.

"The earliest shoes we know of were put in place about 1500," she says. That's more than 500 years ago!

"A shoe is the only item of clothing which takes on the shape of the person wearing it," she says.

"People may have thought that it held something of the wearer's essence even

when it was not being worn.

So it was thought the shoe owner's good spirit would enter the shoe, stay there, and keep away evil spirits that may have wanted to harm the house or the people living in it.

Miss Shawcross says children's shoes are found often.

"It may be that their spirit was considered purer and therefore stronger," she says.

But many children's shoes have been found in the main bedroom, which might have been to help the

mother give birth to healthy babies.

FOOTPRINTS IN TIME

The museum where Miss Shawcross works keeps a record of hidden shoes. The register was started in the 1950s and there are about 2000 entries.

"Two to three finds are reported to me on average a month," she says. "People seem to Google the subject and find out that we keep a concealed shoe register."

The register has finds from all over the UK and other

countries including the US, Australia, India, the Philippines, China, France and Switzerland.

"Although most people say they are not superstitious, in 99 per cent of cases the [shoe] will go back in the building, just in case."

Above, a girl's shoe from 1780, found in a chimney in Hampshire, England with a prayer book from 1781.

Left, women's shoes from 1860–80, found in the floor of the servants' area of a house in Northamptonshire, England. A purse, teaspoons, glass bottle, cotton reel and child's tippet were also found.

Below left, this child's shoe – once red in colour – from 1740–50, was found under the floorboards of Ashley Manor in Gloucestershire in England.

PHOTOS **Northampton Museums and Art Gallery**

The secrets of hidden shoes

❯ A concealed shoe is a boot or shoe that has been deliberately hidden in a building.

❯ Many belonged to children.

❯ People often hid them in chimneys and walls to bring good luck and to ward off evil spirits.

❯ The first documented find of a hidden shoe in Australia was in 1913 in Brisbane.

Child's shoe found in Sydney, Australia

This tiny shoe was found in the attic of a house in the Rocks, near Sydney Harbour, in 2003. The house was built about 1833 but the shoe was probably put there 15 years later. At just 130mm long, it belonged to a very small child.

The house had belonged to George and Mary Hurley. When the Hurleys moved in, Mary had given birth to two children who had not survived. Kids slept in attic bedrooms and because the house had views of the harbour the parents may have felt their children were exposed to evil beings flying across the water. And so the shoe was placed in the roof cavity.

Source: Dr Ian Evans

Below, the shoe hidden in the roof of a house in Sydney near the harbour in about 1850.

PHOTO **Ian Evans**

Lead sentence

'If you live in an old house, there just might be a little bit of magic hiding in the walls.'

Thanks for the knees, Mum & Dad

The injury may also be genetic, or hereditary. Alani's mum and dad both had knee surgery after tearing their ACL.

THANKS, MUM AND DAD

Dr Salmon says doctors used part of the hamstring from Alani's dad to repair her right knee and part of the hamstring from Alani's mum to repair her left knee.

Using parents' hamstrings to repair ACL injuries in their kids is fairly new.

"The hamstrings in adults are larger in diameter and we can use it to make a bigger and stronger ACL for the child's knee," says Dr Salmon.

"It also means we don't risk further injury to the child by using their own hamstring."

Alani is one of 100 children being studied by Dr Salmon whose ACL was repaired by using a piece of hamstring from their parents.

Dr Salmon wants to see if they are less likely to reinjure their ACL than children who had their ACL repaired with a part of their own hamstring.

What is a hamstring?

Hamstrings are muscles on the back of your upper leg that help the knee to bend.

SOURCE **Sports Medicine Australia**

Left, Alani Pond, 18, has had both knees reconstructed using bits of her mum's and dad's knees.

Above, Alani with her mum, Paula, dad, Doug, and their dog Oscar. Oscar has had two knees reconstructed too.

PHOTOS **Jacky Ghossein**

BY **Melissa Davey**

ALANI Pond has a bit of her mum in one knee and a bit of her dad in the other.

When she was 13, Alani tore her right anterior cruciate ligament, often called the ACL. It's like a thick elastic band inside the knee that joins the thighbone and shinbone and keeps the knee strong and stable.

"I heard a crack while I was playing soccer, and after a while the pain was excruciating," says Alani.

"I was really devastated ... I didn't know anyone at my age or level who had an injury like this."

NO SPORT FOR A YEAR

Alani needed surgery and was on crutches for several weeks. Her doctor said she couldn't play sport for a year.

Twelve months later she made a strong comeback, playing soccer with an under-15s team, and won a coach's award.

She also played touch football and won best and fairest.

DISASTER STRIKES AGAIN

But when she was training in Queensland with National Touch Rugby Australia's under-21s development squad in 2015, Alani felt a familiar crack.

"I immediately just knew I had injured the ACL in my left knee," she says.

After more surgery and another year off, Alani worked hard to get strong again and won the 2017 junior NSW state cup with the Parramatta under-18s touch football team.

Alani, who's now 18 and lives in NSW, used the time off from sport to study and to teach herself the guitar, which has become a passion.

TWISTING AND JUMPING

A research physiotherapist, Lucy Salmon, says ACL injuries are rare in children but she's seeing them more often she thinks because more kids play competitive sports at higher levels, and sports that involve twisting or jumping.

Playing safe

❯ Warm up before playing team ball sports

❯ Practise landing safely when hopping and jumping

❯ Do lots of stretches

❯ Don't play sport if you are injured or too tired

3

WHAT IS NEWS?

Why do we see or hear about some things in the news but not others? How do journalists know if a story is newsworthy – important or interesting enough to be on the TV or in a newspaper? And how would you decide if a story should be included in your paper or news show?

There are a few 'ingredients', or principles, that help decide what is news. When we mix all those ingredients together it helps journalists decide how important a story is to their audience. Some stories will include all the ingredients. These might appear on the front page of a newspaper, or open a radio news bulletin. Others may have only a few ingredients and will be published a few pages into a paper or later in the program.

Let's explore some of those ingredients.

Eight news ingredients

1 New

A big clue is in the word 'news'. News is *new*. It might never have happened before. For example:

Riddhi has been elected school captain and will be the first girl to hold that position.

Or it might be a new twist in an ongoing story:

Riddhi has announced that her first job as school captain will be to review the menu for the school canteen.

2 Audience

Reporters need to know their audience. A story that matters to you and your classmates might not matter to the whole of Australia, or the rest of the world.

If your school gets a new playground or outdoor space, for example, it is very important to you and your fellow students. Your recess and lunch times may be completely transformed by the new slides, climbing gym or green open space. But it won't be very interesting to a student over the other side of the country, or in China.

There are national newspapers and programs that cover news that matters to everybody who lives in Australia, no matter where they live. There are also local newspapers and community news programs that provide information about a particular area, such as a suburb or town.

As a journalist you need to think about who is watching, listening or reading to help decide what stories to cover.

Activity time

Think about all the different newspapers, TV and radio news programs or podcasts you know about. If you're not sure, do some research in the library or ask your teachers or parents what they read, watch and listen to. Make a chart like the one below and try to list them under 'National', 'Regional' and 'Local' headings, depending on their audience. Are the stories of interest to the whole of Australia (national), or just your local area (local)? Do they matter to everybody in your state (regional), or just your suburb or town (local)?

National	Regional	Local
Behind the News (TV news)	*The West Australian* (newspaper)	Dungog Community Radio

3 Wow factor

News can be an event that is simply weird or unusual – something you wouldn't see every day. Just like our poor possum in Chapter 1. What have you seen recently that was completely out of the ordinary? How would you report on it?

In Australia we might read about wild bears playing in a backyard in the USA. It's not interesting because it affects us, but because it is so strange and funny to see a bear playing on a swing. This happened to a family in the US state of Connecticut. The video of the bears was shared by news outlets across the globe.

When a new world record is set by Indian sand artists for building the biggest sandcastle ever made, this might also make international news because it is so extraordinary. You don't have to be a sand artist or live in India to find it interesting.

4 Disaster

Natural disasters, like bushfires or cyclones, often make the news especially when they cause a lot of damage or injure many people.

These types of stories are shocking or sad and will matter to people everywhere. An earthquake in New Zealand that destroyed lots of buildings and roads and even killed people is an example (see *Crinkling News* story on opposite page). We all care because we are human and feel sorry for the people affected. Big bushfires in Australia often make the news in Europe, Africa and all around the world for the same reason.

It's the same for terrorist attacks and wars that affect many lives and communities.

5 Powerful people

Powerful people regularly appear in the news. A journalist is much more likely to do a story on what the leader of a country is up to, whatever that may be. They are less

The day the Earth moved New Zealand

PARTS of New Zealand have changed forever after the land shifted up to 11 metres during a massive earthquake.

The 7.8-magnitude earthquake on November 14 was one of the most complex ever recorded – and there will probably be more aftershocks.

A huge clean-up is continuing and two people died because of the quake.

LAND CHANGED FOREVER

The GeoNet science agency said the land moved up to 11 metres along the many fault lines in the South Island disaster zone. This permanently changed its geography.

The quake also pushed up the seabed by as much as two metres along a 110-kilometre stretch of coast that includes the tourist town of Kaikoura.

Warships from the US, Canada and Australia have been taking emergency supplies to Kaikoura, which was the place most damaged. Huge landslides cut the main highway and train lines, but other supplies were taken in by back roads.

About 1,000 tourists were evacuated from Kaikoura by air and sea in the days after the quake but 2,000 locals are still trying to clean up.

RING OF FIRE

GeoNet said the quake ruptured at least four faults and was "clearly ... one of the most complex earthquakes that has ever been observed".

New Zealand is on the border of the Australian and Pacific tectonic plates, which form part of the "Ring of Fire", a string of volcanoes and earthquake zones around the Pacific Ocean.

The earthquake was felt across the whole of New Zealand.

Agence France-Presse

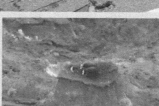

What's an earthquake?

It's when two blocks of the Earth suddenly slip past one another. The surface where they slip is called the fault, or fault plane. When this happens, a whole lot of energy is released and can cause the ground nearby to shake, a bit like ripples on the surface of a pond.
SOURCE: **USGS**

What is "magnitude"?

> It is a measure of the amount of energy released during an earthquake.

> A 2.5-magnitude earthquake or less usually can't be felt by us. Between 7 and 7.9 is considered a great earthquake that can cause lots and lots of damage.
SOURCE: **University of Oklahoma/Michigan Technological University**

Above, earthquake damage to a highway south of Kaikoura on New Zealand's South Island.
PHOTO **Marty Melville/AFP**
Left, these two cows and a calf were stranded on an island made by the earthquake on November 14. The images from Newshub, went around the globe. Newshub reported a farmer rescued them.

A massive earthquake in New Zealand made
news in that country and across the globe.

likely to cover your best friend's every move – unless your best mate happens to be the prime minister of course!

This could also apply to your school. If you were a reporter on your student newspaper, which story would you publish?

Principal refuses to say where she went to university
OR
Student lies about where he went to preschool

29

A school newspaper is more likely to run the first story. The head of a school is going to make news before almost anyone else in the community because the principal is in a powerful position. They set the standards and make the rules. Their decisions affect a lot of people.

A student telling a fib about where they attended preschool really only affects them, so it is not news.

As a student reporter, what would you do if you found out some questionable things about your principal? A group of high school reporters in the USA had to deal with just that.

Principal resigns after student journalists' scoop.

Courtesy of *The Booster Redux*

The Booster Redux student reporters with Maddie third from the left

Student reporters at a North American school discovered their new principal's qualifications – what she studied to gain her position – were not what they seemed. The journalists raised questions about the university the principal said she had attended. They then published an article about it in the school newspaper, *The Booster Redux*.

Days later, the principal resigned. It was big news at Pittsburg High School and even made headlines around the world.

Student Maddie Baden said it showed the importance of journalism. 'Six high school students made a difference in our school and community [by] writing and publishing a story that thousands of people have read all over the world,' she said.

'If you have a story that needs to be told, tell it. If someone is against you telling it, or says you are too young, always stick to what you believe and do not let anyone tell you that you are too young.'

6 Important to society

Journalists regularly cover issues that are important to their community as a whole – to its health, wellbeing and sense of fairness.

For example, stories about people who are badly treated because they are vulnerable – like the elderly, the very young, the sick or the homeless – are often big news. They might affect only a small number of people but they are important because they tell us what we are like as a society. They remind us how we, collectively, treat people who can't always look after themselves.

News stories can give the vulnerable and powerless a voice by telling their stories.

7 Important to lots of people

A storm that ruins your backyard vegetable patch is devastating. It might have taken you a long time to plant, carefully water, weed and grow. While it matters to you, your family – and maybe even your neighbours – it's unlikely to be newsworthy.

But it is definitely news when a cyclone wipes out a whole Queensland banana plantation that provides the fruit to most of the country.

The announcement of a new leader for a global sporting code is news because that person will oversee a sport that hundreds of thousands – maybe even millions – of people play, watch and enjoy. Or it's news if an airport closes due to an erupting volcano affecting everyone who wants to fly in or out from that city or town.

The more people an event or occurrence affects, the more important the story.

8 Truth

A reporter must present an accurate report, stating what really happened. A news report has to be true. It is not your opinion or point of view. Truth is an essential ingredient in news, no matter what the story.

As a reporter, that means:

- don't make things up;
- think about why people are giving you information and whether they are telling the truth;
- ensure information comes from a reliable person or place – often called a source;
- seek information from many sources;

- tell the whole story, including the context or background; and
- double-check the facts.

Journalists have to be mindful of the difference between an opinion and a fact. Using words that make this difference obvious to your audience is essential, as in the example below:

David Duong believes his school, Green Hills Public, is the best in the country at sport = Opinion

Green Hills Public is ranked first in the country for school sport, the official national sports education board has announced = Fact

A journalist needs to be careful about what is true and what is false. Sadly, some people are dishonest, make up stories and try to convince others that they are true. We'll cover more about this in Part III, pages 112–120. But if you do your job as a young reporter – speak to lots of people, research and confirm information and dig deeper – you can avoid being tricked.

4

JOURNALISM THROUGH THE AGES

Reporters have been around for a long time. Journalism in its most basic form – telling people something new or important – goes way back in history.

Spoken news

Spreading and sharing news has always been essential to human survival. According to Mitchell Stephens, author of *A History of News* and professor of journalism at New York University:

> 'I don't think there ever was a society that did not exchange news. The human urge to hear and to tell news is so strong for good reason – for their genes to survive our ancestors had to be alert to what was going on around them.'

Word of mouth was the first, informal way news was shared. The need for something more organised became stronger as people started living in stable communities.

Farming helped humans settle in one spot where they could grow crops and raise livestock.

Around 8000 years Before Common Era (BCE) it became someone's special task to run around and tell others what was going on. 'As societies started to grow larger, informal news systems weren't good enough and things got more organised,' Professor Stephens said.

The first 'journalists' were messengers who spread information through villages and towns by physically running many kilometres to deliver news.

As more and more people moved to towns and cities, town criers delivered spoken messages to residents who mostly couldn't read or write. The town criers – who would yell or 'cry' out announcements to a gathering of people in a street or marketplace – often had to rely on their memory.

Written news

The first known writing system used symbols carved into clay tablets. It was a slow process, but an important step towards recording information more permanently.

Writing developed over the years to include letters and words. Material, cloth, paper and tools to write were created, which led to handwritten documents, books and texts. Information could now be shared with less and less reliance on a messenger's or crier's memory.

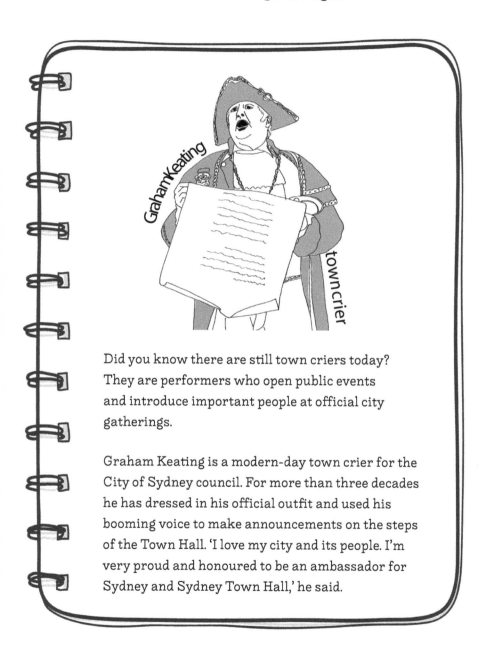

Graham Keating

town crier

Did you know there are still town criers today? They are performers who open public events and introduce important people at official city gatherings.

Graham Keating is a modern-day town crier for the City of Sydney council. For more than three decades he has dressed in his official outfit and used his booming voice to make announcements on the steps of the Town Hall. 'I love my city and its people. I'm very proud and honoured to be an ambassador for Sydney and Sydney Town Hall,' he said.

Let's fast forward to 59 BCE. At this time, written news could be shared with lots of people all at once. In ancient Rome, official notices detailing political, official and social events – the *acta diurna* (daily acts or events) – were made public for the first time by order of political leader Julius Caesar. This meant handwritten authorised notices were displayed in public places where everyone could see them.

News over time

8000 BCE	Messengers and criers
2500 BCE	Clay tablets
59 BCE	Public news summaries in ancient Rome
618–906 CE	Block printing for sharing news in China
1240s CE	Metal moveable type in Korea
1450 CE	Printing press first used
1600s CE	First newspapers
1920s CE	Radio
1940sCE	Television
1990s CE	World Wide Web

From Professor Stephens' *A History of News*

Printed news

Printing completely revolutionised the way we shared information. The exact same words could be printed over and over again to produce all kinds of texts – from fictional stories, poems and bulletins to religious texts.

Printing was invented in China. An official news-letter, the *tipao*, was produced using 'block print-ing' during the T'ang dynasty in the years 618 to 906 Common Era (CE) for the elite groups in the Chinese empire.

Block printing involved carving characters or letters out of a block of wood, covering them with ink and pressing the block onto cloth or paper. It took a long time to do!

Moveable type – where individual letters could be shifted around to form words – sped things up. Raised backward letters were arranged, coated in ink, then pressed onto paper to print the information the correct way around. By the 13th century, Koreans were able to make moveable type using metal.

Two centuries later, a German named Johannes Gutenberg designed a printing press using metal moveable type and a simple machine to print. The press made it possible to produce texts like books and pamphlets on a really large scale, making exact copies for lots of people to read.

The first regular newspapers were published using printing presses in Europe around 1605, which is why the news media is still sometimes called 'the press'.

Gutenberg's printing press.

A 'free press'

The idea of a 'free press' – where journalists can go about their work without being controlled or restricted by powerful people – has a long and bumpy past. It is still a battle today.

Throughout history, people in authority have tried to stop or control what information could be shared with the general population. They have often succeeded. As early as 1502 rulers in Spain forced all printers to check with the government or church before publishing.

Authorities in America were strict too. 'The first newspaper published in the Americas in 1690 only published one edition because it was quickly shut down by authorities because it said nasty things about the king of France and about England's Native American allies,' Professor Stephens said.

Beyond ink

Last century, new inventions again changed how information was shared. Short, silent news bulletins were projected onto cinema screens. These were sometimes used for 'propaganda' – governments made short films to convince people to agree with their decisions, especially during times of war.

News programs were first heard on radio in the 1920s and seen on television from the 1940s. For the first time in history, radio and TV allowed audiences to hear and see politicians and public figures, even if they were hundreds of kilometres away.

This meant news could be shared quickly and there was less need to wait for a paper to be printed. Television and radio allowed news to be delivered 'live' to an audience, so a reporter could explain what was happening as it occurred.

Then along came the World Wide Web in the 1990s, which allowed news and information to be spread rapidly via the spoken or written word, photos, graphs and videos. Audiences can now interact directly with news by commenting, sharing, clicking and even contributing to stories in real time.

5

WHY NEWS MATTERS

Journalism is important to a healthy society and democracy. It informs, uncovers hidden truths, entertains, connects people and keeps a check on power and the powerful. It is also a reliable record of current events. In fact, it's sometimes said that journalism is the 'first draft of history'.

According to Michael Schudson, a professor of journalism at Columbia University in the USA, there are three key reasons why journalism matters.

1   'It builds a shared community. Journalism tells a community about itself. People in families care about one another not only because they usually live together but because they talk together about themselves. They put their lives into words. The words describe, comment on, celebrate, and challenge the family's common life and help make just-being-together into a truly shared life. Journalism does something like this for towns, cities, regions, nations.'

2   'It tells us where we stand in time. Journalism
     tells people how things are changing. Fast!
     Faster than we think! And journalism – that
     focuses so much on what just happened, what
     is happening, what is trending – keeps us up
     with where we are in a larger, ever-shifting
     world. We can't know who we are without
     knowing where we are in time. Journalism
     helps.'

3   'It keeps powerful people on their toes.
     Journalism tells people in positions of
     power that someone is watching. Someone
     remembers what they pledged to protect
     and whom they promised to serve. Someone
     remembers and calls this to public attention
     when the person in power has betrayed the
     trust of the people. Democracy can't work
     without this.'

Journalism for communities

News helps build a shared community. It is hard to feel
part of something or care about an issue if you don't
know anything about it. Think of a school project that
bored you at first. Then as you researched the topic and
gathered some facts you suddenly cared. News can spark
that too. Learning that your local park is being used as a

dumping ground for litter might inspire you and neighbours to come together to do something about it.

News can also be lifesaving. During disasters like bushfires, people use the news to stay informed and safe. In a health crisis, journalists interview experts and share the latest public health information so people know what to do and how to stay well.

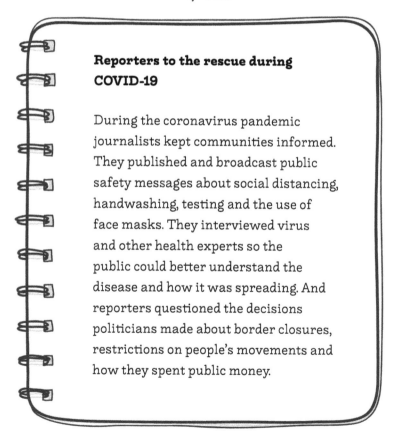

Reporters to the rescue during COVID-19

During the coronavirus pandemic journalists kept communities informed. They published and broadcast public safety messages about social distancing, handwashing, testing and the use of face masks. They interviewed virus and other health experts so the public could better understand the disease and how it was spreading. And reporters questioned the decisions politicians made about border closures, restrictions on people's movements and how they spent public money.

Somebody should celebrate what's great about your community and journalists do that, too. It's important to hear who won the local weekend soccer game, or read about a student who won a prize, or find the date of an upcoming carnival. We don't want to just hear about the bad stuff!

A community newspaper

THE MONTHLY RAT

Audrey E was nine years old when she and her friend Noah started *The Monthly Rat*. The newspaper was for kids, by kids and covered the latest news and events in the rural Victorian city of Ballarat. They published 14 editions in total.

'For the first issue we (me, Noah, my younger brother, and his younger sister) wrote all the articles about things going on locally – a fire in a restaurant we happened to walk past, a new gelato shop review, and a story about a massive park that just opened,' Audrey said.

It was fun being a reporter but she also saw the importance of local news. 'Writing *The Monthly Rat* was a way of telling kids what was going on around them in a way that they would understand and want to read. Because it was written by other kids. Not by adults who wrote like adults,' she said.

'And people need to know what is going on around them because if they don't they might put themselves or

The Monthly Rat

A newspaper for children, by children

Issue 3 DECEMBER 2016

Big smash on corner of Mair and Doveton streets!

On the 16th of November a minivan crashed into a traffic light pole on the corner of Doveton and Mair streets.

We knew about this because it was on the radio. The radio person said that no one should go near it, so (of course) we drove straight there. But that is what any good journalist would do!

The man driving the minivan was killed, but not because of the accident. He suffered a medical conditon and drove into the traffic light. The medical condition could have been a heart attack, I don't know!

Minivan after the crash.

When we got there the van was all smashed up and on the back of a tow truck. The was one ambulance, three police cars and one fire engine. The people from the fire engine weren't helping at all, they were just drinking coffee and might of been talking about ladies!

Audrey E

Firemen drinking coffee.

Mum unplugged our TV

In the middle of September my family stopped watching the television. We were aiming to not watch it for two months.

I didn't think it would affect me much because I used to only watch tv on Fridays and Sundays.

The only other screens in our house are the two computers and Mum and Dad's phones. George and I were still allowed to have half an hour of Minecraft on Friday, Saturday and Sunday.

Now we have finished the two months, the results are that we sometimes forget that we own a tv, we don't watch much anymore, (only on weekends) and if you asked me what my favourite tv show was I couldn't tell you because I don't have one!

Instead of watching television I read books, did maths and built lots of cubbies. I think that you should try to go without tv for two months!

Audrey E

The Monthly Rat was a local newspaper for children, by children.

47

others in danger. To have a local newspaper, just for the area you live in, you can find out much more about the community around you. Whereas with a newspaper that is national I highly doubt it would mention a small local event where you live.'

Audrey thought covering local stories was a great experience. 'It was pretty fun to report on events in the community. Although sometimes it was a bit scary, going up to random people and interviewing them, but it was worth it because you got a good story out of it. Also, you could find out interesting news before anyone else because you were the one reporting on it.'

Audrey E

Journalism for democracy

Government and society work best and are fairest when people make informed decisions about their lives. Journalism helps them do that.

In a democratic country, citizens have certain freedoms, rights and responsibilities. One of those rights is to vote in elections and help decide who will run the nation, state or council. The power of politicians and leaders is 'checked' by the people. If the citizens don't like what the government is doing, they can vote for someone else at the next election.

But to know who to vote for citizens need to know what is going on – they need to have access to information that is clear, true and fair so they can make educated decisions. That's where journalists come in. They report on what politicians are or aren't doing without taking sides.

Reporters do this by reading and researching the laws politicians make, watching who they speak to, and assessing whether they are being honest. Journalists also act as a watchdog for the people by checking on everyone in power, including police, judges, religious leaders and rich business people.

That's why journalists need to be able to do their jobs freely – even if those in power don't like what they're writing or saying. If they are scared or if they get in trouble for doing their jobs, reporters might not be able to find the truth.

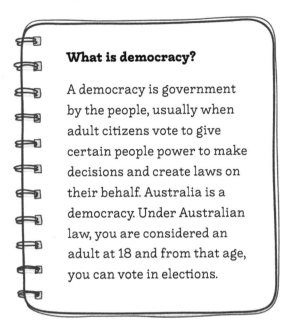

What is democracy?

A democracy is government by the people, usually when adult citizens vote to give certain people power to make decisions and create laws on their behalf. Australia is a democracy. Under Australian law, you are considered an adult at 18 and from that age, you can vote in elections.

Journalism for change

Reporters can uncover secrets that lead to big changes and help people lead better, safer lives.

Once a reporter tells the public about an abuse of power or wrongdoing, everyone knows about it and can demand action.

News reports can lead to:

- changes in government;
- a powerful person losing their job for wrongdoing, or not doing enough;
- new rules or laws to protect vulnerable people and places;

When kids' rights are taken away, bad things happen

BY **Darren Moncrieff**

WHEN ABC television's Four Corners program showed images of boys in the Don Dale juvenile detention centre in Darwin being badly treated by their guards, Australia was shocked.

The Prime Minister, Malcolm Turnbull, was so upset he ordered a royal commission to investigate what had happened to the boys, some as young as 13.

Since the footage was shown on national TV, the Northern Territory government minister in charge of prisons, John Elferink, has been sacked.

But what do the kids in Darwin think about it?

"When I first saw it, I couldn't sleep

that night," one local teenager said.

Another said: "It's sad. He was so young. My mum didn't like it as well."

The North Australian Aboriginal Justice Agency, which is helping two of the boys who were in Don Dale, has been talking to school students about the law.

The agency tells them about their rights if they get into

trouble with the police.

"Some of these boys [in the Four Corners program] aren't angels, but even if you do something wrong and break the law everyone has basic rights," says James Parfitt from the justice agency.

"And when these are taken away bad things start to happen."

Right, Dylan Voller, 19, one of the boys whose treatment in juvenile detention was shown in the ABC's Four Corners program, wrote this letter after the show aired. His lawyer, Peter O'Brien, released a copy of it to the public on Twitter.

You still have rights, even when you are behind bars. ILLUSTRATION **Christopher Downes**

CHILDREN BEHIND BARS

BY **Dhana Quinn**

SOMETIMES children do bad things – they might hurt someone or steal something – and end up in detention.

But kids can end up in juvenile detention centres for something that you might find surprising – like not wearing a helmet when riding their bike

Professor Paula Gerber, from Monash University in Melbourne, says one of the reasons why children end up in detention is because their family is poor.

"If children commit an offence they might be given a fine," she says. "If they can't pay the fine, then they may be imprisoned.

"Children have been picked up by the police for not wearing a helmet when riding their bicycles and been given a ticket.

"But their grandparents or parents

couldn't pay the fine so the child was locked up in detention for 21 days, for example."

Professor Gerber says Australia needs to stop punishing these children and try to find out why they are committing crimes in the first place.

"Is it because we don't have good quality education? Is it that they don't have a good quality family life?

"There's always a reason children are behaving in a certain way."

Who is in juvenile detention?

> Even though Indigenous Australians make up a small percentage of our population, they make up a much bigger percentage of people in children's and adult jails.

> For example, in New South Wales, Indigenous young people make up just five per cent of the state's population aged between 10 and 17 years – but they make up 43 per cent of young people in detention or being supervised by the prison system.

> In the Northern Territory, Indigenous young people make up 45 per cent of the population aged 10 to 17, but 95 per cent of those in detention.

Source: Australian Institute of Health and Welfare, Youth Justice in Australia 2014-15

This article is about an ABC news story
that led to government action.

- big companies fixing mistakes or paying for crimes;
- punishments for bad behaviour; and
- improvements in how communities work.

Kids in jail

In 2016, journalism exposed the fact children were being very badly treated in prison. A news story about kids in a Northern Territory juvenile detention centre – a jail for people aged under 18 – was broadcast on ABC television. Through the *Four Corners* report, the public found out some guards were hurting boys held at the centre. It shone a light on those in power – the guards and others responsible for young people's detention in the Northern Territory. It also raised questions about how children accused of crime, or found guilty of one, should be managed.

The story led to immediate action by the Australian government. A huge public investigation – a royal commission – was set up to look closely at what happened and advise authorities on how to fix the problems.

This is the power of journalism at work.

PART II

ON ASSIGNMENT

6

WRITING A NEWS STORY

Now that we know about the job of a journalist and why it matters, we can get down to business and put a story together!

There is a formula reporters use to get the basic information needed to write a cracking news story. The magic recipe is: **W+W+W+W+W+H**. Each letter represents an essential question that needs to be answered to ensure the audience gets all the facts.

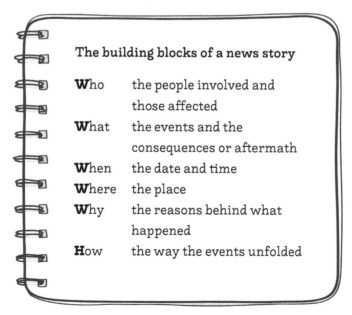

The building blocks of a news story

Who   the people involved and those affected

What   the events and the consequences or aftermath

When   the date and time

Where   the place

Why   the reasons behind what happened

How   the way the events unfolded

Okay, why don't you give it a go?

KEEP OUT

You head to your favourite skatepark – skateboard or scooter in hand – only to find it taped off and a sign saying, 'Keep Out'.

To write a report about this for your local newspaper, you'd need to answer those six essential questions to help your readers understand the situation. They would want to know why it was shut, when it will reopen and who is affected.

Who?

You need to find out who made the decision to close the park. You should also check who will miss out on skateboarding while the park is shut.

What?

It sounds obvious, but you need to name the skatepark and point out that it can't be used. You could describe the tape roping it off, tell people exactly what the sign says and explain what facilities are at the park, like a half-pipe and a toilet block.

When?

When the park closed – including the day, date and even the time – will all be of interest to your readers. It's even more important to tell them when it will reopen, or if it's been shut permanently.

Where?

The location, such as the street and suburb, will help people identify the skatepark.

Why?

Explaining why the park is closed will likely be the most interesting part of your story. Was someone hurt or is something broken? Is the park being upgraded or demolished?

How?

How was the decision made to shut the skatepark? Were kids and others living nearby asked for their opinion? Were young people asked to stop skateboarding while a council worker strung up the tape? And if the park's being upgraded, how will it be fixed or improved?

As you get answers to these questions and gather more information, you will have even more queries. For instance, if the park's being shut permanently, where is the nearest skatepark? Who can skaters contact to make it clear there's a need for a local skatepark?

Activity

You've had a look at a made-up scenario. Now let's look at a real news story. Read these three paragraphs and try to find the five Ws and one H.

Human icy poles take the plunge

In Antarctica right now it's not only freezing cold, it's also dark because the sun never rises above the horizon.

But that didn't stop Antarctic expeditioners from celebrating the shortest day of the year – known as the winter solstice – by taking a dip in the freezing waters at Australia's research stations on June 21.

With the air temperature about -33.5°C and the water temperature just -1.8°C, 15 of the team at Davis station plunged through a hole in the ice for the traditional midwinter swim.

Human icy poles take the plunge

BY **Lara van Raay**

IN Antarctica right now it's not only freezing cold, it's also dark because the sun never rises above the horizon.

But that didn't stop Antarctic expeditioners from celebrating the shortest day of the year – known as the winter solstice – by taking a dip in the freezing waters at Australia's research stations on June 21.

With the air temperature about -33.5°C and the water temperature just -1.8°C, 15 of the team at Davis station plunged through a hole in the ice for the traditional midwinter swim.

SUNSHINE COMING SOON

Davis station's leader, Kirsten le Mar, says midwinter's day is the halfway point for expeditioners wintering on the continent and it's a highlight of the Antarctic calendar.

"After three weeks of darkness, [June 21] marks the beginning of longer days in Antarctica, although it will still be 19 days before the sun starts to peek above the horizon here at Davis," says Dr le Mar.

The tradition of midwinter celebrations dates back to more than a century ago, and is celebrated by expeditioners of all nationalities.

There are 68 expeditioners living and working in Antarctica and on sub-Antarctic Macquarie Island this winter.

A Davis expeditioner takes an icy plunge for the traditional midwinter swim in Antarctica. PHOTO **Robert Bonney/Australian Antarctic Division**

ANSWERS

Who?   Fifteen Antarctic expeditioners.

What?   Swimming in freezing waters.

When?   The winter solstice / June 21.

Where?   Australian research facility Davis station, Antarctica.

Why?   Celebrating the shortest day of the year with a traditional midwinter swim.

How?   Plunged through a hole in the ice.

Did you find the five Ws and one H? Read the entire article to find even more details.

7

SOURCES OF INFORMATION

You need sources to answer your **W+W+W+W+W+H** questions. These include people, books, reports, websites and sometimes media releases. It's essential for a reporter to know how to find useful, trustworthy and accurate sources of information, often very quickly.

It's also good to have more than one source for each story. If, for example, you rely on information from a single interview, you'll only have one person's account or point of view. But speaking to many people builds a more complete picture of what happened. This will also help you decide what is a rumour or untruth and identify information that doesn't make sense.

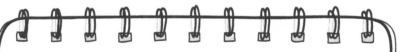

Sources of information

- people
- books
- journals
- websites
- reports and studies
- media releases

- photographs and images
- infographics
- videos, footage and audio recordings

What is a source?

Imagine a friend tells you that your school will be officially renamed Hogwarts.

How would you go about investigating whether this was true or not? Who, or what, could be useful sources of information?

Let's brainstorm.

- Ask your friend where they got the information, then follow the trail to get to the original source.
- Check with the school principal.
- Contact the education department.
- Find reports or research papers about school name changes.
- Look at author JK Rowling's official website for any announcements.
- Do an internet search to see if a real school has ever been renamed Hogwarts.

These are all possible sources of information.

Name and explain your source

As a reporter, you must tell your audience where you got your information. If you interview someone you need to include the person's name and title, plus where they work or the suburb, town or city where they live. If you use details from a report, name the report, say who wrote it and when it was written or published. The same goes for information from a book, website or even pamphlet. Acknowledging your source is known as attribution.

Point of view

Your audience will better appreciate your story if they understand the sources' points of view. This gives context to their opinions and statements.

After reading the sentence below in a news story, what would you think about the Green Team?

> Apple High School student Andrea Rossi said the Green Team basketball side was rubbish.

We know Andrea is a student at Apple High, but we don't know why she thinks the Green Team is terrible. Now let's add some more information about Andrea that will help a reader understand why she holds that view.

> Apple High School student Andrea Rossi, who is the captain of the Blue Team, said the Green Team basketball side was rubbish.

Ah, Andrea is the captain of a rival basketball team. She could be saying the Green Team is bad because she wants everyone to think her team is better! Providing people's titles and explaining where they work, who they represent or where they are from, allows your audience to put comments into context.

Supplying context helps readers and listeners make up their own minds about the information. It's not a journalist's job to tell the audience what to think, just to provide them with the facts. And that includes explaining where your sources are from.

Give credit

As a reporter you are telling other people's stories as best you can. You can't pretend their work or words are yours. You must give them credit by naming them.

You should never copy other journalists' news stories. When you do your own research and interviews you can be sure what you are reporting is correct because you have checked the facts.

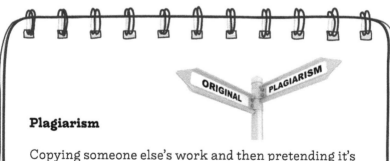

Plagiarism

Copying someone else's work and then pretending it's yours is called plagiarism. It is dishonest and it will get you in trouble. Plagiarism is never okay – not at school, not at university and not in journalism.

Trustworthy sources

Reporters want facts and a true account of what happened from their sources. But how do you decide if you can trust your source?

We will cover how to be an information detective in Part III, pages 112–120. For now, we're going to discuss the basics – sorting out reliable from untrustworthy sources.

It comes down to you as the reporter. You need to be curious and not believe everything you see or hear. This means asking yourself some essential questions.

- Who is putting out the information? Does the person or organisation have a good reputation? Can they prove they are who they say they are? Is there a way of contacting the people behind the study or website? Have you ever heard of them? What else have they said?
- Why is someone sharing this information? Do they have something to gain?
- Who else is talking about this topic? Are there multiple sources saying the same thing?
- When was the information shared or published? Is there a date? When was the article or website updated? Is there more-recent information about this topic?

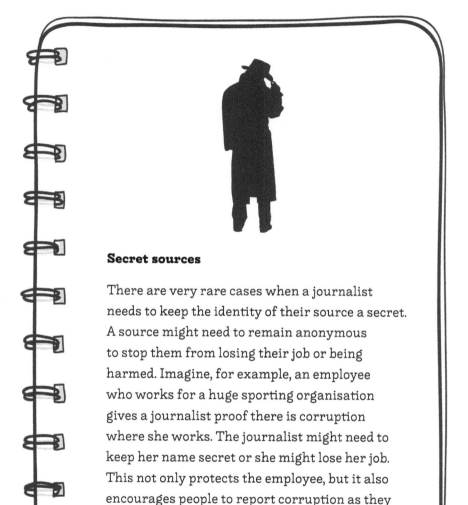

Secret sources

There are very rare cases when a journalist needs to keep the identity of their source a secret. A source might need to remain anonymous to stop them from losing their job or being harmed. Imagine, for example, an employee who works for a huge sporting organisation gives a journalist proof there is corruption where she works. The journalist might need to keep her name secret or she might lose her job. This not only protects the employee, but it also encourages people to report corruption as they know journalists will protect their identity.

A source especially for reporters

A media release is a source of information written especially for journalists. It's also called a press release or news release.

Newsrooms are sent media releases 24 hours a day, seven days a week. They can come from companies, individuals, governments, police departments, fire chiefs, sporting bodies, book publishers or theatres – basically from anybody who wants journalists to pass on their views or messages to the public.

But just because something is in a media release doesn't mean it should be in a news story. Most media releases end up in the recycling bin or deleted folder. But some will have useful, even essential, information.

For example, a police press release might detail road closures during a flood, which could be included in a news story to help keep communities informed and safe.

8

INTERVIEWING

Reporters interview lots of different people every day. When interviewing, it helps to be confident, friendly, respectful and, most importantly, nosy! The way you talk to people and ask questions has a big impact on how much information they give you.

Let's begin with the basics.

Talking to people you don't know well can make you feel nervous or shy. Having a clear idea beforehand of what you want to ask will give you confidence. Write down and rehearse your questions so you're well prepared.

Your interviewing starter kit:

- Introduce yourself and name your news outlet.
- Take careful notes or recordings, but always ask permission before recording.
- Pay attention to details by checking the spelling of the person's name and, if relevant, their age.
- Get the facts.
- Aim to get more information than you need.

- Be safe – if you are interviewing someone outside a safe environment, such as a school or your home, you need a trusted adult with you.
- Never interrupt a police officer, firefighter or other emergency worker when they are doing their job.

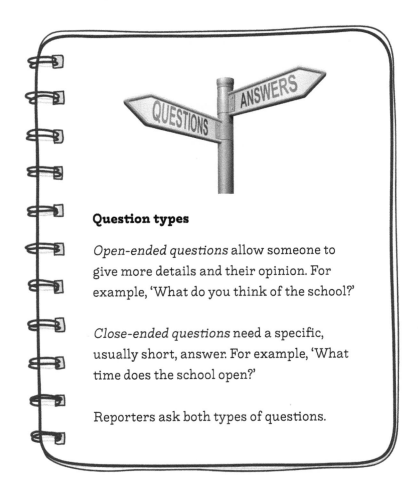

Question types

Open-ended questions allow someone to give more details and their opinion. For example, 'What do you think of the school?'

Close-ended questions need a specific, usually short, answer. For example, 'What time does the school open?'

Reporters ask both types of questions.

Try it out

Let's return to the rumour about your school being renamed Hogwarts and add some specifics (see page 61).

SCENARIO

A friend tells you that your school, Treetop College, is going to be officially renamed Hogwarts. Your brother has shown you three social media posts about it and an art teacher has started wearing a Ravenclaw scarf!

You decide to interview the school principal for the student newspaper, *Street News*. What types of questions would you ask? What information do you want?

Practise with a classmate or friend before tackling the real interview.

You: Hello, my name is [insert your name] and I am writing a story for *Street News*. Do you mind if I ask you a few questions?

Principal: Yes, you may.

You: Can I record the interview, please?

Principal: Yes, certainly.

You: May I please have your name and the spelling of your name?

Principal: My name is Basil Parsley, spelt B-A-S-I-L and P-A-R-S-L-E-Y.

You: What is your official title?

Principal: I am the Principal of Treetop College.

You: Thank you. I would like to know if this school is planning to change its name from Treetop College to Hogwarts?

Principal: No, absolutely not.

You: Why do you believe some students think the school's name will change?

Principal: I can't speak for them. But at the end of last year the school council did talk about the school's name. Hogwarts was never discussed as an alternative to Treetop.

You: What other names did you talk about?

Principal: Maybe Hilly High, but I can't be sure. In any event, we decided there was no reason to change the school's name.

The discussion about possible different names was not very long. If you want to look at what we explored, you can look at the minutes – the official record of the meeting in November. You can ask the librarian for copies of them.

Based on your interview with the principal, you can now be fairly certain there are no plans to change the school's name to Hogwarts. And you now know you can find further information in the minutes – the school council meeting records. This will give you two reliable sources of information – the principal and the minutes – to put together a short news story.

When you write your article for *Street News*, you can include some interesting and important pieces of information.

- Let your readers know Treetop College will not be called Hogwarts (source: principal).
- Inform students the school council did consider a name change, but this was ruled out (source: council minutes and principal).
- Provide details about the names discussed (source: council minutes).

Interviews on air

There is more than one way to interview people. The way you talk to someone for a written news story is different from how you interview them for radio, television or podcasts. Their voice – and probably yours – will be heard by the audience in broadcast news stories, so the message needs to be clear.

In broadcast news there are two main ways to present interviews. You can produce a package with lots of other voices and images, or feature a longer conversation involving just you and the person you're interviewing.

Broadcast news

Broadcast news is traditionally stories transmitted or delivered via radio or television. These days, news can also be broadcast — seen and/or heard — through the internet on news websites.

Packages

Broadcast news stories can be presented as a 'package'. This includes 'grabs', or snippets, of footage and audio recordings taken from interviews. There might be only one person featured or there could be many.

The audience won't hear or see the full interview between the source and the reporter in a package, just a small part of the recording. Packages are very common in TV and radio news bulletins.

On the next page is an example of a script for a short radio news story. Read it aloud and make up voices for the different parts or try it with your classmates. You could record it too, using a school or home computer – or a smartphone if you have access to one. It helps to hear how you sound so you can improve your broadcast voice!

The sentences in bold are the 'grabs', or quotes, from the people interviewed.

News reader:	Hundreds of students protested today in the city centre. Ake Karlsson has more on this story.
Ake Karlsson:	Students have gathered outside Parliament House to voice their concerns about wearing school ties. Seventeen-year-old student organiser, Roo Kang, from Town High says ties are not needed: '**It's annoying running around at lunch with something around your neck.**' State Police officer, Nil Blue, says no one was arrested: '**It was a peaceful protest of around 1000 students.**' Private Education Association boss, Kel Ley says ties are important: '**They help create school pride.**' Students say they will return to Parliament House next year if there is no change. Ake Karlsson, Radio News.

Interview-only stories

Sometimes news and current affairs programs feature one longer interview, normally with someone powerful or well known. The audience hears or sees a whole conversation between the reporter and the person being interviewed. These might form part of current affairs television shows like *Dateline* on SBS and *The Project* on Channel 10, or longer podcasts and radio programs, such as *Hack* on the ABC's triple j. They give your audience the chance to hear from one person in more detail about their own lives or a big issue.

For example, if a fellow student was evacuated from their home due to a bushfire, asking them what happened and how they felt would be an interesting longer interview for a school podcast.

You need skill and practise to do a great interview, so we decided to ask an expert. Avani Dias is a journalist and the host of triple j's *Hack*.

Avani Dias

Avani Dias's top five interview tips

1   'Take your audience on a trip. Just like a great
    book or movie, a good interview should take
    us on a journey. Start with a question that'll
    make your audience stick around and build
    it up to end with something revealing about
    your interviewee.'

2   'Listen. You can plan an interview as much
    as you want but you need to be able to listen
    to someone's answers and ask them questions
    based on what they say. Don't be afraid to go
    off script!'

3   'Have a conversation. When you're chatting
    to someone at school, it's not just you asking
    questions and them answering. Bounce off
    your interview subject and react to their
    answers the way you would in a normal
    conversation.'

4   'Don't let them walk over you. Politicians are
    masters at avoiding your questions so don't
    be afraid to cut them off and ask them to give
    you a straight answer. If they keep dodging,

then you can flag it to your audience by saying something like, "Okay, you're clearly not answering the question, let's move on" so they know the politician is being useless!'

5   'Stay confident. There are a million different ways you can do an interview and there'll be people who aren't into your style. Always listen back to your interviews and think about how you can make them better, but remember you're behind the mic because you're good!'

9
RECORDING AND PHOTOGRAPHING

Tools

Being a reporter is like being a detective. You need to gather evidence and record it to prove your story is true and to help your audience understand it. The evidence can include photographs and video footage of what you're describing, as well as audio recordings of interviews.

You need the right equipment to record that evidence. And that means you need the help of a trusted adult too.

Newspaper reporter

- Small audio recorder, dictaphone, smartphone or tablet for recording interviews
- Notepad
- Pen or pencil

- Computer, laptop or tablet
- Smartphone or camera for taking photos

Radio reporter

- Audio recorder
- Microphone
- Headphones
- Notepad
- Pen or pencil
- Computer, laptop or tablet for editing
- Audio editing software

Television/video reporter

- Smartphone, tablet or video camera for recording footage
- Notepad
- Pen or pencil

- Computer, laptop or tablet for editing
- Video editing software

Photojournalist

- Smartphone, tablet or camera
- Notepad
- Pen or pencil

There's a lot of technology out there to make it easy to capture images, footage and audio. If you work in a professional newsroom you are given this equipment.

Finding the right software

There are plenty of computer software programs and apps for recording and editing. Some are free and there are also expensive professional options. You'll need to investigate with a trusted adult to find software that you can easily operate, works on your computer, and fits your budget. Programs often come with guides and tips.

But starting your own news outlet means discussing what you need with a trusted adult and looking into how much you or your school has to spend, or what you have available already.

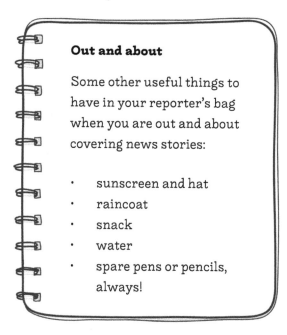

Out and about

Some other useful things to have in your reporter's bag when you are out and about covering news stories:

- sunscreen and hat
- raincoat
- snack
- water
- spare pens or pencils, always!

Using the tools

When recording or photographing someone for a news story you should follow the same rules we talked about for interviews.

- Get their permission.
- Check the spelling of the person's name, their job title and who they work for or where they live, so you can identify and describe them.
- Take note of the time, date and place.
- Check with a trusted adult whether you need permission to record or photograph in a particular area or place.

Capturing footage and images takes a lot of time. Even then, you still have a long way to go. You might need to give yourself time for editing and sorting. It's useful to have a good filing system for your recordings so you can find what you need quickly. This means labelling your recordings with the subject, date and time.

Be careful to edit honestly. You don't want to cut out part of someone's sentence and change the meaning of what they were trying to say in the process. You must be fair in how you tell the story of what happened.

A powerful image

Photographers and photojournalists play a very important role in producing news. An image helps tell a story by showing the audience what is happening while the reporter describes it. Sometimes a photo is the story! You should first get permission from the person or people

CrinklingNEWS

TUESDAY MAY 24 2016   7

Farmer's maze solves erosion puzzle

> **66 The dust was so thick it was like a fog that blocked out the sun and sky and made it hard to breathe or see. 99**
>
> *Brian Fischer, farmer*

ENVIRONMENT

BY **Stephanie Osfield**

EARLIER this year, maze-like trenches appeared on Ashmore White Suffolk Stud Farm, north of Adelaide. From the air, they look like mysterious crop circles or symbols from ancient Greece.

But they did not appear overnight and how they formed is no mystery.

It took a week for farmer Brian Fischer and his two sons to plough the patchwork pattern of trenches into 400 hectares of his land. The point? To stop soil erosion caused by bushfire.

"We guessed how far apart to place them, but each rectangular patch is about three acres wide, the trenches are about 10 centimetres deep, and each strip of trenched and untrenched land is about five metres across," Mr Fischer says.

"The ridges direct and funnel the wind so whichever way it blows it is at 90 degrees, so it can't easily pick up the soil."

FIRE AND DUST

Winds of up to 200km/h fed flames that travelled 1.5 kilometres a second, devastating Mr Fischer's farm on November 25 last year.

More than 80,000 hectares of farmland burned in just four hours, and 87 homes were lost.

"We were lucky we didn't lose our home, but the fire cooked and flattened our land, turning our farm into a dust bowl," he says.

This caused dust storms as wind swept the topsoil up into the air.

"The dust was so thick it was like a fog that blocked out the sun and sky and made it hard to breathe or see," Mr Fischer says.

As a result, the farm could no longer grow barley or wheat or house its usual 1,000 head of sheep.

UPROOTED

"In recent decades, climate change has led to more bushfires and heavy rainfalls which disturb the roots of trees and grasses, causing the top layer of soil to be washed or blown away," says Professor Will Steffen, a climate change expert from the Climate Council and Australian National University.

"Cutting down less trees and planting more trees are important ways to prevent and stop soil erosion."

New farming techniques can also help, such as direct seed drilling where a seed is dropped into a hole drilled by a machine, leaving topsoil alone.

HEALING THE LAND

Mr Fischer learnt the trench technique from his dad, also a farmer, who used it in the 1930s and 1940s during a drought.

The trenches have saved our soil which is now becoming healthy enough to replant," says Mr Fischer.

"As we plough each new section to sow seeds, we level out the land and the trenches disappear."

Above, the ridges on the Fischer farm designed to stop soil erosion.
PHOTO **Supplied**

How great is this photo!?

you are photographing. At school you will need to check with a teacher.

An image can bring news to life. In the story on page 83, a farmer and his sons north of Adelaide in South Australia spent a week ploughing a maze of trenches into 400 hectares of their land. They did it to stop the soil blowing away after a bushfire.

Without the photograph it would be much harder for readers to imagine what this looked like. It gives them a bird's-eye view of the stunning maze.

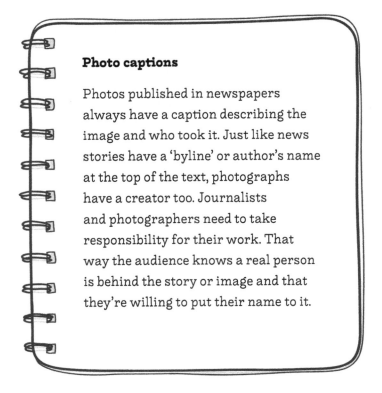

Photo captions

Photos published in newspapers always have a caption describing the image and who took it. Just like news stories have a 'byline' or author's name at the top of the text, photographs have a creator too. Journalists and photographers need to take responsibility for their work. That way the audience knows a real person is behind the story or image and that they're willing to put their name to it.

Parts of people's homes and properties fell into the sea at
Collaroy in Sydney following a huge storm in 2016.

Photo: Jacky Ghossein

This one dramatic photograph allows the audience to
immediately grasp the story. It shows the damage caused
by a massive storm where huge waves pounded the coast
causing it to erode. Parts of homes, including balconies,
pools and yards, fell into the sea.

What makes a great news photo?

Jacky Ghossein has been a news photographer for more
than 20 years. She took this photo of the properties falling into the sea. We asked her what makes a compelling
photo.

'A great news photo captures the moment or event and stops the viewer in their tracks, engages them, tells a story, and leaves them wanting to know more,' she said.

Jacky Ghossein's perfect photo

1   'Make sure the sun or light is behind you when you take a photo. You want the light shining on the person or object. Outside, the best natural light is in the early morning or late afternoon. Use a lamp or sunlight through a window inside.'

2 'Think about everything you can see through the lens or on the screen. Look at what's in the background. Check the area around your subject is clear. You don't want a photo of someone with a pole or tree appearing to stick out of their head!'

3 'Think about how you frame and balance your photograph. For example, you could use a window or door frame to create a natural border. Look at where the land or sea meets the sky and make sure it's straight. Buildings and walls should be vertical, not tilted! And try not to cut off people's feet or hands.'

4 'Experiment with how you take pictures. Don't always stand directly in front of your subject. Try moving around before taking the photo. Change your point of view. Crouch down low or safely climb on something to get above your subject. Get really close to them or far away.'

5 'Talk to the person or people. Ask them about their day. The more you chat and engage with someone, the more relaxed they will be and this will show in your photograph.'

6 'Practise and practise some more! Have your camera handy whenever you can. Over time, you'll get more comfortable and improve.'

10

TIME TO FILE!

Before you file your first story, we need to back up a bit. We need to create a newsroom. We're going to pretend you work for your school's student newspaper, *The Insight*.

Your physical newsroom is a classroom with a sign on the door that reads, '*The Insight*: for students, by students'. Inside there are 15 of the paper's front pages tacked to the wall. Your proudest journalism moment is displayed there – your first front-page scoop, a story about exams being postponed last year due to a computer meltdown. There are 10 tables arranged in a semicircle, each with a notepad, pen and a name card on top.

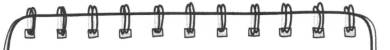

Scoop
Journalists are always trying to get the story first, before any other reporter. A 'scoop' is a news story that no other journalist has.

The Insight has 10 staff members.

- One student editor decides which stories to cover and where they are published in the paper.
- One supervising editor, a teacher, who helps the students run the paper.
- One student subeditor checks spelling, facts and names, plus writes headlines or story titles.
- Four student reporters: two cover general news, one covers sports, one covers arts and entertainment.
- One student artist draws illustrations and comics.
- One student photographer takes photographs of people and events.
- One graphic designer, a student or adult with the skills to design the layout – how the stories and images look on the pages.

The Insight is an electronic newspaper so it's emailed to the school community, rather than printed, in the final week of every term. The deadline for stories to be filed by each reporter is the second-last Friday of term.

That gives the subeditor a chance to check the stories, the editor time to place the stories in the paper and do a final read through, and the supervising editor time to email the edition out to students, parents and teachers.

We'll go into more detail about how to set up and run a student newspaper in Part IV, pages 154–163.

Deadline

A deadline is when a reporter's story has to be completed and filed, or sent, for editing.

Getting the story

It's lunchtime on the second-last Monday of term. You head to *The Insight* newsroom to check how the latest edition is going because it's only a few days until deadline.

As you walk into the classroom, your editor calls out: 'Great timing!' You learn two Year 6 students were playing soccer at Green Park on the weekend and they found a bag of diamonds. 'Their class teacher is Mr Schmidt and he's on yard duty,' the editor says. 'Can you please find him and ask permission to interview at least one of the students. Get all the details you can. This is a front-page story!'

The editor asks the photographer to attend the interview with you. The supervising editor has printed out a media release from the official police service website.

Remember, this is Monday and your deadline is Friday. That's a lot of pressure.

Check your toolkit: pen, notepad, audio recorder to record interviews, laptop or tablet to write the story.

Remember the six essential questions: **W+W+W+ W+W+H**. You'll need to answer all of them.

You approach Mr Schmidt and he says Nikoda Khalil, one of the students who found the bag of diamonds, will be happy to talk to you. The other student is a bit shy and doesn't want to be interviewed but is happy to be named in the story. Mr Schmidt will make sure Nikoda stays back in the 6B classroom at recess on Tuesday for the interview.

The next day, armed with your audio recorder, notepad and pen, you head to the 6B classroom. It goes something like this.

Interview with Nikoda Khalil

You: Hi Nikoda, thanks for letting me interview you about the bag of diamonds you found! Can you please spell your

name, tell me how old you are, and
confirm what class you're in.

Nikoda: Nikoda Khalil, I'm 12 and I'm in 6B.

You: So, what happened?

Nikoda: I was playing football with Dean Smith
at Green Park on Sunday. Dean kicked
the ball into the bushes. When I looked
for the ball, I found a small red bag. I
called Dean over and we opened the bag
and saw the diamonds. We didn't think
they were diamonds though; they kind
of looked like bits of clear glass. But we
thought we'd better check and ask my
mum just in case.

You: When did it happen?

Nikoda: We went to the park around 2 o'clock
on Sunday, so some time after that. As
soon as we found the diamonds we went
home and showed my mum and she
drove us to the police station.

You: Where exactly were the diamonds found?

Nikoda: They were on the ground, under a bush
at the park.

You: Apart from being red, what did the bag look like?

Nikoda: It was a small soft bag with a yellow drawstring tying it shut.

You: What did the police say when you handed it in?

Nikoda: The police officer said, 'Thank you, you are very honest kids.' And then said investigators will try to find the owner.

Police media release

On Sunday, June 15 at approximately 2pm two children found a bag of diamonds at Green Park in Suburbville.

The children, both aged 12, handed the bag into Suburbville Police Station at 4.15pm.

The diamonds are estimated to be worth $50,000.

Police are calling for the owner of the diamonds to contact Suburbville Police Station.

Story tips

- Start with an attention-grabbing first sentence.
- Make sure it's accurate.
- Name your sources.
- Double-check the facts.
- Check spelling of names and places.
- Take your readers on a journey as you write the story.

You have two sources – Nikoda and the police. You can write your story. But where to start? How do you organise the information?

Think quickly. What is the most interesting part of the story? Write your first sentence, one that will grab your readers' attention.

Then write a story that allows the reader to easily follow what happened. Get all the details in there – the who, what, when, where, why and how.

You have to tell the story in 200 words because that is how many words can fit in the space the editor has created for this story in the newspaper. Go!

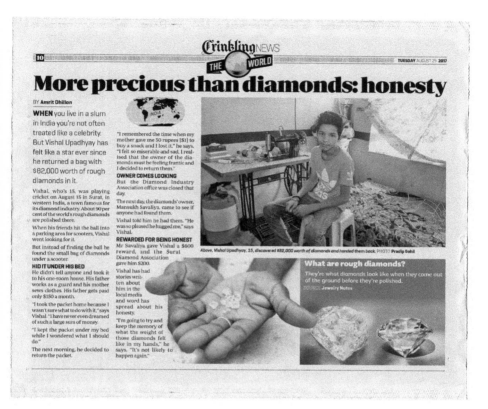

Honesty pays.

This pretend story actually happened in real life. A teenage boy called Vishal Upadhyay in Surat, India found $82,000 worth of diamonds in a bag when he was playing cricket one day.

By reading this real story you might get some ideas for how to write your own news story.

Writing for radio or podcasts

If the school produced *The Insight* as a podcast instead of an e-newspaper, how might you write the diamond discovery story as a script? Try this yourself, then check how you went by comparing it to the script we prepared. Take a look back over the interview with Nikoda and the police media release to give you ideas.

News presenter:	Welcome to *The Insight*, a news podcast by students, for students. First to our top story. Two students from our school found a bag of diamonds at Green Park on the weekend. Kayode Quill reports.
Kayode Quill:	A game of soccer turned into a huge find for Year 6 students Nikoda Khalil and Dean Smith. Nikoda says she was looking for the ball when she saw a red bag. 'I called Dean over and we opened the bag and saw the diamonds. We didn't think they were diamonds though, they kind of looked like bits of clear glass.' The pair, with Nikoda's mother, took the diamonds to Suburbville Police Station.

Investigators say the diamonds are worth around $50,000. Police are calling for the owner to contact them.

Finding your own stories

At this point you might be asking yourself, 'How do I find a story on my own?' News is happening around you all the time; you just need a nose for it!

Everyday news

You don't need to look too hard to find a story. An interesting or exciting event may be happening nearby right now. In Part I, pages 24–34 we talked about ingredients that make a story newsworthy, including whether it's *new information*, matters to your *audience*, is about *powerful people*, affects *many people*, is *bizarre or strange*, or reminds us that we're all human and *connected*.

A festival, parade, sporting event or circus in your neighbourhood could be worth covering. You can find out they're happening from advertisements on the street, flyers, media releases and by hearing people talk about them.

Fires, floods, accidents and other emergencies will also matter to your audience. You might see them happening yourself, hear about them from friends or family or find out from the local fire or police station.

Keeping an eye on the weather forecast is useful, especially if it's especially hot and dry or there's been an unusual amount of rain.

Knowing who the community leaders are in your area is important if you're going to keep your audience informed. Who is your local council mayor and member of parliament? They often make announcements about new programs, buildings and other projects.

Reporters keep a diary of upcoming events. For example, the school sports carnival or annual play should be in your diary. If your school council is looking into how it will spend money next year and plans to release a report in August, making a note of the date in your reporter's calendar will help you remember.

The key to finding news is being curious. If you overhear your mum talking to a friend about how they rescued an injured kangaroo joey from the side of the road, that could be a big story for you.

Tip-off

Occasionally, someone will contact a journalist or news outlet to give them information for a story. A parent might email your student newspaper to say their son is competing in a community debating competition next week. Or a local resident could contact a reporter to say the nearby playground has been graffitied.

Time to file!

When journalists are given a tip-off they need to investigate the claim to see if it is accurate and worthy of a news story. We'll go into more detail about how to be a news detective in Part III, pages 103–111.

Contacts

A journalist's contact book is their best friend – it's full of names, email addresses and phone numbers for people who'll help them find stories, confirm facts and provide more information. As a student newspaper reporter, who would be in your contact book?

Write down some people who you think would be useful to include. We've given you some suggestions to get you thinking.

My Contact Book

- Student representative council members
- Sports team captains
- Principal
- Local council members
- _____
- _____
- _____

The office numbers for local politicians and key community leaders and organisations are important contacts if you cover stories in the community. If you're a specialist reporter you should have contacts in the area you cover, such as club leaders if you're a sports reporter.

And make sure you keep the contact details of people you interview. You might need to speak to them again.

You are now well on your way to becoming a journalist! But before you start your own news outlet, let's do some investigating.

PART III

HOW TO BE A NEWS DETECTIVE

11

SLEUTH AT WORK

It's time to get out the magnifying glass. Before you can call yourself a reporter, you need to understand where information comes from, how it's created, how it's understood and what's done with it. Journalists are critical thinkers. That means turning over every bit of evidence, examining it, and then making an informed decision about its value.

We looked at sources in Part II, pages 60–66, but now we need to dive deeper. How do you tell the difference between a rumour, a lie and a fact? When does a statement become an opinion? Is it okay to have various perspectives, or points of view, on the same event?

People have different ideas about the world. These are formed by family and friends, school, culture, heritage, religion, community, even government. All these influences on your life affect the way you see information and how you pass it on. And that is the same for every person in the world.

Being aware of this helps us appreciate other people and respect their views, even when we disagree. It helps us understand our own perspectives and lets us sort through and share information in a fairer, truthful way.

To be *media literate* involves knowing the difference between reliable and unreliable sources, being able to fact-check claims and spot fake news and advertisements.

Developing these skills is an important part of being an engaged and informed citizen in the 21st century.

Who said what and why?

All forms of knowledge come from somewhere. Information includes any and all details about a situation, person, thing or event. But someone has to create that information, whether it's written, spoken, in a report, part of a video or in a graphic.

As a news detective you have to find out who created it, try to understand why it was produced and identify the target – who the creator wants to reach with the information.

These are clues to help us understand all messages. And their meaning can change depending on their context.

Let's do a simple exercise to get you into detective mode.

Think about this image. Who might have produced it? Why would they want to share it? We've included some possibilities below. If you think of more reasons, you can add them to the end of the table.

Who?	Why?	Target
Pet store	To get people to spend money and buy a dog	Kids, families, people looking for a companion
Dog rescue centre	To find a home for an abandoned puppy	Animal lovers, kids, families
A friend	To show people they have a new puppy	Friends
Animal rights group	To encourage people to get their pets desexed	Pet owners

As you can see, this one image could mean many things to different people depending on who published it and why. Understanding the reason and context behind its creation helps you decide what to do with it.

Emotions also play a role in how we respond to information. How did the puppy make you feel? Some information can make you emotional. You might cry at the end of a sad movie, get angry when you hear a puppy has been abandoned or be happy when your team wins the grand final. Is the person who created the information hoping to get a reaction? Would others feel the same as you? Who might not? And why?

A critical thinker is aware of what's happening behind the scenes. They think about who created the message, what the creators are trying to achieve and who they are trying to reach. Critical thinkers are less likely to be fooled and more likely to know how to interpret the message.

Different hats

Imagine you have lots of different hats in your bedroom – caps, top hats, wide-brimmed sun hats, hard hats, beanies and more. To help you process different information, we're going to pretend to put on a different hat to match each message type.

Choose a different hat for each of the following information types. If you like, you can write 'Entertainment',

'News', etc. underneath the types of hats below.

- Entertainment
- News
- Friends and family
- Advertisements

Information is produced to inform, influence, distract, persuade, entertain, sell, or even insult and be mean.

Noticing the reasons behind different messages can help you make sense of them. A purpose is matched to each type of information on page 108. You might like to draw or name a hat for each.

Type of information	Purpose
Personal	entertain, convince, celebrate
News	inform
Advertisement	sell something
Research	inform, explain, convince
Community announcement	inform, persuade
Entertainment	amuse, distract
Rumour	insult, distract, persuade
Opinion	influence, convince

When you watch an advertisement during your favourite television program, you could pretend to put on your 'ad hat'. Watch the advertisement knowing it was created to get you to buy a product or service, like new shoes or a trip to a theme park. An ad isn't going to tell you what's bad about the shoes or park, and it won't tell you about other options.

A movie needs an 'Entertainment hat'. It might be creative, funny or sad. But you wouldn't rely on it to make serious decisions about your life.

News, on the other hand, should be well researched and fact-checked. Wearing your 'News hat', you could learn about what is happening in your community or the world around you.

When you talk to family and friends you change hats again and use everything you know about that relative or mate to make decisions about what they say.

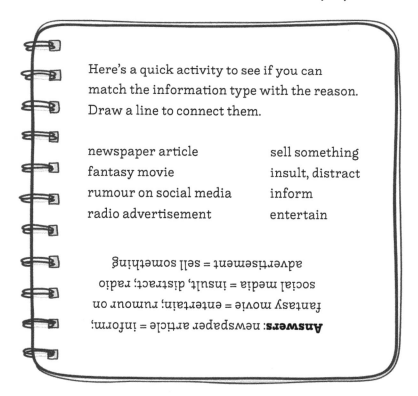

Here's a quick activity to see if you can match the information type with the reason. Draw a line to connect them.

newspaper article	sell something
fantasy movie	insult, distract
rumour on social media	inform
radio advertisement	entertain

Answers: newspaper article = inform; fantasy movie = entertain; rumour on social media = insult, distract; radio advertisement = sell something

Advertising versus news

Advertising is selling something to an audience. The idea is to get as many people as possible to buy a product or service, or to support a cause.

HOW TO BE A NEWS DETECTIVE

CrinklingNEWS

A faster than light drive on the solar system highway

Heather Zubek *straps herself in for a ride through the solar system without leaving the road.*

THE map showed that we had reached Coolah, a tiny town in central NSW. But there beside us was the planet Neptune.

A 3D model sat on a huge billboard just metres away.

On the billboard were interesting facts about this blue planet, including that Neptune has the fastest winds in the solar system - winds up to 1,500km/h.

Neptune and its billboard are just one part of a project designed to

Faster than the speed of light

If you're travelling in your car at 100km/h along Solar System Drive, you're "virtually" moving through space at a million kilometres a second, more than three times the speed of light.

SOURCE: **Solarsystemdrive.com**

teach tourists and kids all about the solar system and show them just how big the universe really is.

The virtual Solar System Drive is a model of the solar system that is 38 million times smaller than outer space.

HEADING TOWARDS THE SUN

The 3D planet models are on roads in central regional NSW leading to the "sun", the 37-metre Anglo-Australian telescope dome at Siding Spring Observatory just outside Coonabarabran.

The real sun is more than 1.39 million kilometres wide but when it is scaled to the size of the dome at the observatory, the model of Pluto, less than 200 kilometres away, is the size of a billiard ball.

LEARNING ON THE ROAD

A Coonabarabran astronomer, John Shobbrook, came up with the idea in 1992, hoping people might develop an interest in astronomy and science.

"Being immersed in the solar system in this way will truly give students and tourists

a feel for the vastness of space and the fragility of the tiny planets, especially planet Earth," he said at the official opening of the drive in 2007.

"The families taking the drive find it informative and we find many want to know more about the other roads that lead into Coonabarabran," says Aileen Bell, from the Warrumbungle shire council.

Around the globes

Each planet is moulded from fibreglass, and ranges in size from five centimetres to 3.9 metres in diameter.

"Just today I noticed two small buses of international students at the Saturn planet board just south of Coonabarabran."

There are five drives - from or near Gulgong, Dubbo, Tamworth, Merriwa and Moree - and they all start with "Pluto" and end at the "Sun" in Coonabarabran.

Mercury Venus Earth Mars Jupiter Saturn Uranus Neptune Pluto

News is a truthful telling of the facts that is meant to inform the audience, not to convince or sell something.

Newspapers and broadcast programs often include both news and ads. Ads help pay for the news produced by journalists. Companies and organisations pay money to a news outlet to advertise in the paper or on the program. But it's important the audience knows the difference between ads and news so they can approach and consume the information wearing different hats.

LEFT This page from *Crinkling News* is split in two. The top half is a news article about the solar system. The bottom half is an ad for a charity organisation's advent calendar and is labelled 'advertisement' in the bottom right-hand corner of the page.

12

TRUE OR FALSE?

Fake news

We hear the term 'fake news' a lot these days. But what is it?

Fake news can be false or misleading stories that seem real. They're often spread to influence the way people think about politics or ideas.

Let's take a look at an example of how fake news might look in real life.

Imagine you are running for class president. The person running against you is Rippon Ripstir and he is not playing fair. He wrote a note saying that you cheated in a Maths test, even though you didn't. He photocopied the note and put a copy in everybody's locker.

Now every time you ask someone to vote for you, they ask you about cheating. You didn't cheat. Rippon made it up, but you spend lots of time denying it instead of talking about why you want to be a school leader and what you want to achieve.

It's annoying. It's dishonest. And it might even mean you don't get elected.

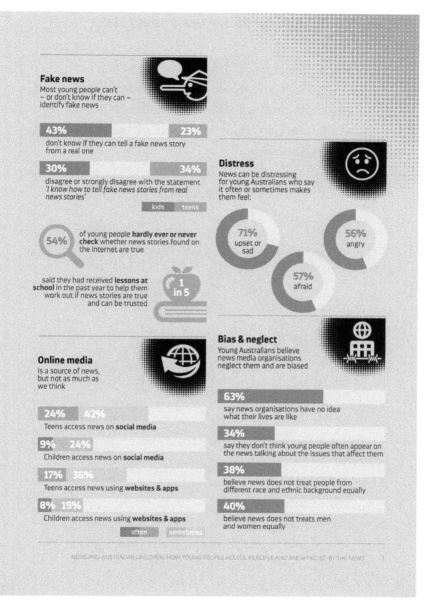

Fake news
Most young people can't
– or don't know if they can –
identify fake news

43% **23%**
don't know if they can tell a fake news story
from a real one

30% **34%**
disagree or strongly disagree with the statement
*'I know how to tell fake news stories from real
news stories'*

kids teens

54% of young people **hardly ever or never
check** whether news stories found on
the internet are true

said they had received **lessons at
school** in the past year to help them
work out if news stories are true
and can be trusted
**1
in 5**

Distress
News can be distressing
for young Australians who say
it often or sometimes makes
them feel:

71%
upset or
sad

56%
angry

57%
afraid

Online media
is a source of news,
but not as much as
we think

24% **42%**
Teens access news on **social media**

9% **24%**
Children access news on **social media**

17% **36%**
Teens access news using **websites & apps**

8% 19%
Children access news using **websites & apps**

often sometimes

Bias & neglect
Young Australians believe
news media organisations
neglect them and are biased

63%
say news organisations have no idea
what their lives are like

34%
say they don't think young people often appear on
the news talking about the issues that affect them

38%
believe news does not treat people from
different race and ethnic background equally

40%
believe news does not treats men
and women equally

Did you know? A 2017 survey on news and Australian children found
one third of young people aged 8 to 16 said they could not
tell the difference between 'fake news' and real news.

Western Sydney University, Queensland University
of Technology and *Crinkling News*

Sadly, there are people like Rippon in the real world. Some people produce fake news stories to disrupt elections, because they think it's funny or because they are paid to be dishonest.

Why lie?

Here are some reasons why someone might create fake news.

- To make money
- To seek attention
- To convince people to think a certain way
- To convince you to buy something
- To cause a distraction
- To stop someone getting elected
- Because they think it's funny

Content

As a news detective, you need to be able to spot clues and decide what is true or false. The people named or quoted in a story is one clue. Examining who these people are, where they work, what their job is and whether other people recognise them is a good start.

Another clue is whether the story is fair. If there's only one point of view it could be biased, or favouring one perspective over all others. A news story that leaves you with more questions than answers could also be suspect.

You should look closely at who created the story, why they created it and who they are trying to reach.

Quality

Unreliable information sometimes even looks dodgy. The quality of the writing or presentation can be a give-away. Alarm bells should ring if there are lots of spelling mistakes, the sentences don't make sense or there are random words in capital letters. If you find yourself reading something and thinking, 'My baby brother could write better than this', you're right to be suspicious.

The same goes for videos. If the captions in a news video are misspelt or seem strange, you should check where it came from and whether there is reliable evidence elsewhere for what the story is claiming.

Real news is not lonely

If you're ever unsure about the facts in a story, see if you can find other sources reporting the same news.

If well-known news outlets have covered it too, this is a good sign. Finding the person who originally made the claim is even better. Then you can judge the information for yourself.

Tricksters versus misunderstandings

Not all incorrect information is meant to trick you. Friends, family and even trusted adults will sometimes believe a rumour or lie and pass it on to others thinking it is true.

They don't mean to mislead people. But as a critical thinker you can help them. Ask them where they got the information, who created it and why they believe it?

This is very different from people who deliberately spread false information.

Fact-checking

As a news detective, you can investigate claims or statements to see if they are accurate.

Let's get some help from a professional fact checker. Sushi Das works at RMIT ABC Fact Check, a partnership between Melbourne's RMIT University and the Australian Broadcasting Corporation (ABC).

What does a professional fact checker do?

'Fact checkers listen to well-known people who speak about matters of importance. These people might be politicians, businesspeople or even celebrities talking about things like climate change, poverty and refugees, or how to stay safe from a nasty virus.'

Sushi Das

'Fact checkers choose a statement or claim made by these people and check whether it is accurate. They do research by reading reports, examining data, talking to experts or looking at historical documents. Then they decide whether the claim is accurate, false, nearly accurate or even a complete lie. And write up their research so that it can be published on a website.'

What can student reporters do to fact-check a claim?

'It's all about being a critical thinker and being alert. That means not automatically accepting that information you hear or read is accurate. Instead, you should make an effort to check something before repeating it or sharing it. Anyone can do simple fact-checking by asking the following questions: Who is making the claim? What is the purpose of the claim? Who is the intended audience? And what are others saying about the topic?'

How could students fact-check the following statement from the made-up Dogs Rule Association? *'Tens of thousands of Australian children are allergic to cats.'*

- 'Be sceptical. Be wary about why Dogs Rule might be making such a claim. Are they making this claim to be helpful or is it in their interest to say this?'

- 'Ask questions. Who are Dogs Rule? Do they even exist? If so, what's their main purpose? Do they have a history of criticising cats? Who might be their intended audience?'

- 'Be a detective. Find out if other people are saying anything about this claim. What do other dog organisations say? Is anybody accusing Dogs Rule of making an inaccurate or exaggerated claim?'

- 'Check the numbers. Find reliable sources that give you the data that show how many children have allergies, then check how many of these children have allergies to cats. Is it exactly "tens of thousands" or close to that number?'

13

ONLINE INVESTIGATOR

The internet is full of fabulous information that can help with research for news stories. But not everything you read or see online is reliable. Some people set up fake websites, make up stories and spread rumours. Why? For the same reasons we talked about in Chapter 12 – to influence, distract, sell, entertain or just cause trouble.

Luckily, there are plenty of great resources to help you find trustworthy online sources to inform your news stories. Australia's eSafety Commissioner and the Alannah & Madeline Foundation have advice on online safety, fake news, media literacy and privacy. Overseas websites, such as MediaWise, Common Sense Media and Civic Online Reasoning, are also useful. For information on the above websites and more, see Resources on pages 189–190.

Domains

To help separate reliable online sources from fake ones, it's important to know your domains. Internet addresses help you understand who is behind a website. The final letters of the address will tell you the kind of website it is and where it's located.

Common Australian ones are listed below.

.com.au	company or business
.net.au	network, often private enterprise
.org.au	community, religious or non-profit organisation
.edu.au	education providers, such as schools and universities
.gov.au	government website

The domain or online territory is a clue about why the site exists. For example, .com.au is most likely a business that wants to sell something and make a profit. Its website is used to promote products or services and could also be an online shop, so people can buy things.

If the company sells gardening gloves you won't see on its website: 'Our gloves are not that great.' You're much more likely to read: 'Best gardening gloves ever!'

While you can get information from many websites, in general .gov.au and .edu.au sites will publish information based on more reliable or official research. But you should still do your detective checks no matter what the web address.

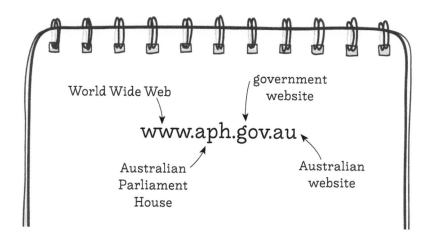

Online checklist

There are hints on every website to help you decide if it's genuine or useful. Open up a website you are allowed to visit and run through the checklist below. Ask yourself the following questions.

- Are there spelling mistakes?
- Does the web address, or URL, look odd?
- Is there a way to contact the person or people behind the website?
- Are there dodgy advertisements or too many ads?
- Is there a date on the information or website?
- Do the links on the website work and do they take you to a proper site or page?
- Do other websites you know link to this site?
- Does the web page provide evidence for claims it makes and does it name its sources?

www4.hapynews.com/myurl/clickhear

5 June, 2002

PIGS FLY ACROS FARM!

Many people reported seeing larje pink pigs flying over farm yesterday. The pigs look extremly hapy. They land graciously nearby in feild. Everyone clapped loud. CLICK HERE FOR MOORE!!!!

CLICK HERE TO WIN $1m!!!

Enter your name and address to win all the prizzes.

Watch out for incorrect spelling, lots of ads, dodgy ads, bad sentence structure and odd website addresses.

Watch out

Keep it offline

You should always be wary about how much personal information you share online.

The Australian eSafety Commissioner says to keep information like your school name, address, suburb and birthday to yourself to avoid online scammers and hackers. The more personal information you share online the easier it is for tricksters to piece it all together and target you. Check your social media, web browser and phone privacy settings with a trusted adult. And don't share your passwords with anyone.

Security software for your devices, like tablets, laptops and smartphones, is also a good idea as it protects your information.

Always think carefully before you click, open or download something. Nasty computer viruses and malware – malicious software – can infect your computer, do a lot of damage and, in rare cases, even spy on you.

Journalists are often known in the wider community because their name is in the newspaper, or people see them on television or online. As a reporter, it's important to keep your 'public' profile separate from your private life. For example, if you were covering a story about a lost pet in your street you wouldn't include the fact that you live on that road. That would give people a clue to your address, which is private.

Verification

Confirming whether something is true or not is one of the most essential jobs of a reporter. We discussed how to fact-check claims in Chapter 12, pages 117–120 and the same ideas apply online.

- Who created the information?
- Why?
- Who's it for?
- Are the claims backed up with evidence?
- Is the same information published elsewhere?

Imagine a big sports story like the AFL grand final. It would be hard to convince people in an online post or news story that the Sydney Swans had won if every other news outlet in Australia, plus the official AFL website, reported that Richmond had claimed the title.

Photos can lie

There are other ways to trick you online. And not all of them are as easy to check as the AFL grand final champions. Photographs and images can be altered using editing software. The change might be small, like adding a filter to a smartphone photo of your friend at the beach. The filter might make the day look warm and sunny when it was actually cold and cloudy.

A brand-new image can also be created by combining parts of two different photos. For example, someone could take a photo of a cow lying on the grass and put it on top of a photo of a car bonnet.

The new image looks like the cow is lying on a car! You might be tempted to write a news story about this because it's so unusual and funny, but you'd need to

investigate first to find out whether it really happened. Remember, your audience trusts you to tell them the truth.

Technology, special effects and good acting also make almost anything possible on film. But the same technology used to entertain can also be used to deceive us, even if it's just as a joke.

Even the best journalists can sometimes be deceived by fake news, scams, clickbait and fake photos or videos. Learning to be a critical thinker by testing the evidence and questioning what you see or hear is key to avoiding untruths and tricks.

14

PERSPECTIVE AND OPINION

Perspective is how you see and interpret the world. But your point of view depends on where you are standing, where you come from and the people in your life. For example, if you draw the number six on the ground with chalk, it will look like either 6 or 9 depending on where you stand.

Your life experiences – where you live, how you are raised, where you go to school and your religion and culture – help shape the way you view what happens around you.

Think about what influences your perspective and write a list. How about your friends? Your family? Are you a member of a religious group? What sports do you play? What are your family traditions? Where do you live? What is expected of you in your culture?

Below are some possible influences on your thinking.

- family
- friends
- culture
- society, like rules and government
- school
- work
- religion
- events
- experiences
- location
- community

As a reporter you need to be aware of your own perspective as well as the points of view of sources and people you interview. This will help you sort through information to get to the facts, present news in a fair way and be a respectful and tolerant person.

Investigating motive

Imagine you are writing a story for a student newspaper about a decision to cut down a big old tree in front of the school.

With teacher permission you interview fellow students about whether they think it's a good idea.

Vladimir, in Year 7, thinks the decision is terrible. His family has lived over the road from the school for three generations and his mum remembers climbing the tree's low branches when she was little.

Kartika, in Year 9, is very happy it will be removed. Magpies nest high up in the tree and every spring they swoop her and her friends while they eat lunch.

The students' perspectives on the decision to cut down the tree are different because they have different experiences. Vladimir is influenced by his mum and family history, while Kartika is affected by the magpies' behaviour in spring.

Neither of them is wrong nor right. But as a reporter you need to respect both views and make sure they are fairly included in your news story.

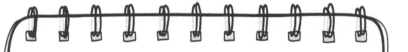

Activity

Try writing the first part of a news story with the information above, including the decision to cut down the tree and how different students feel about that. Give equal weight to both opinions without taking a side.

Opinion or fact

A fact is something that is true and can be proven with evidence. An opinion is someone's view or belief. A journalist needs to know the difference and make it clear to their audience which is which.

Let's examine some examples of fact and opinion to get you thinking.

Soccer involves kicking a round ball = Fact

Soccer is the greatest game on Earth = Opinion

An official government report found football is the most-played team sport in Australia = Fact

Football boots are really comfortable = Opinion

An emotional statement about soccer is not a fact. You could not write a news story stating that soccer was the greatest game on Earth, even if you personally believed that. But you could write an opinion piece and argue your case.

Play fair! Sportswomen deserve equal pay

The NSW women's cricket team, the Breakers, has become the first fully professional female team in Australian sport. This means they will now be able to earn enough money from cricket to support themselves, without having to work in other jobs as well.

Amber Garth, *aged 12, from New South Wales, says it's time men and women earned the same in all sports.*

The pay difference between the two genders can vary in professional sport.

Many people seem to believe it's fair that in many sports women don't receive as much money as men.

But I, and many others, believe it's unfair. We should try to find a way to make pay for athletes equitable, regardless of gender. And we should also strive for women's sports to be just as valued as men's sport in terms of pay and viewers.

Why do women in general still earn 83 cents in comparison to a man's dollar?

In sport, most of the pay gap is to do with sponsorship. The highest paid female soccer athlete in the world, American Alex Morgan, makes only about half a million dollars a year. The highest paid male in soccer, in contrast, earns more than $50 million.

A reason women should definitely be paid just as much as men is because women actually have to work twice as hard for their professional non-contact sporting success.

Women have wider hips than men – which means the femur, or thigh bone, is on an inward angle; women have less physical capacity than men, and women's muscle mass is lower. A woman's shoulder and upper body strength has about 20 per cent lower capacity for power than a man's.

No one would dispute that female athletes work as hard as their male counterparts. But sport is no longer just sport. It is a business, and the workers get paid for how much money they make for the business owners.

If female sports made as much money as male sports, then of course the athletes should be paid the same – or in a few cases, perhaps more.

In the sports world, pay equality is growing in some areas, such as tennis.

As professional sport brings in a ridiculous amount of money in general, we should find a way to invest more in our female athletes and pay them the same as their male counterparts.

Sportswomen deserve to receive pay parity. Women put in the same number of hours, sweat and, arguably, sacrifice more when taking part in elite sport. Pay packets, rewards and recognition should reflect that.

The US soccer player Alex Morgan in an Olympic women's qualifying game. PHOTO **ISI Photos/US Soccer**

This text opposite is called an opinion piece. The newspaper states this at the top of the text. But you can also tell because of the language used and the way it's written.

The author, Amber Garth, is arguing professional sportsmen and sportswomen should earn the same amount of money.

Amber is writing in the first person, which means she's using 'I' to tell the story – it's her perspective. Journalists normally write in the third person, using 'he', 'she', 'it' and 'they' to tell a story about someone else.

Amber says: 'But I, and many others, believe it's unfair.' The word 'believe' is another clue that this is her opinion. She also uses emotional words like 'deserve' to mount her case, such as: 'Sportswomen deserve to receive pay parity.'

Even if an opinion piece uses lots of facts and evidence to support an argument, it doesn't make it a factual news story. An opinion piece is written to provide an argument for or against a position. Often, it's written to persuade readers to support that position. It's not meant to be a balanced news story that weighs up the evidence from all sides.

The important thing is to make sure the audience knows the article is an opinion piece. That way, they can put their 'Opinion hat' on!

15

INDEPENDENT
AND FAIR

There are basic principles that guide journalists as they go about their work – a set of values so reporters know how to behave when they do their job.

News organisations sometimes have their own special rules for reporters. There are also standards set by groups looking after workers in the industry. For journalists in Australia that organisation is the MEAA, or Media, Entertainment & Arts Alliance. As a member of the MEAA, reporters agree to follow these rules.

MEAA Journalist Code of Ethics

MEAA members who work as journalists commit themselves to:

- Honesty
- Fairness
- Independence
- Respect for the rights of others.

'Honesty' might seem obvious. Most people would want a journalist to tell the truth. But including it in the code of ethics makes it very clear what is expected.

Dr Denis Muller is an ethics expert who works at the Centre for Advancing Journalism at the University of Melbourne.

'There should be a clear set of standards for jobs like journalism,' he said. 'Otherwise, what was right or wrong would come down to what the individual journalist thought was right at the time. That won't do.'

According to Dr Muller, the key ethical and moral guidelines for journalists to follow are truth in storytelling and treating people decently.

Truth

'Being truthful in journalism means getting your facts right and presenting them in a way that fairly reflects all aspects of the subject matter,' Dr Muller said. That means putting the facts in context and giving them meaning.

'Being truthful also means being open-minded, willing to change what you reported when the facts change,' he said. This can happen when new information comes to light or details evolve over time.

Respect and fairness

Reporters also need to be honest as they research and when they interview people.

'It means being upfront about the fact that you are a journalist and that you want to include them in your story,' Dr Muller said.

Balance

As a student reporter it's your job to produce a story that is as complete and as honest as possible. For example, if a massive new building was being constructed in your town, it would be a good idea to talk to those who like the idea. You'd also want to chat to people who don't want the building.

But not all sides of an argument are equal.

Dr Muller said balance means following the weight of evidence. A good example is climate change. 'The overwhelming scientific evidence is that climate change is real and is caused by human behaviour,' he said. So, giving equal time or space in a news report to those who disagree is irresponsible because the evidence clearly shows climate change is real.

Your stories should include lots of different voices and opinions, but you need to be responsible.

Right of reply

If you publicly name a person or organisation, they have a right to respond or defend themselves. For example, if you want to publish an article in your school newspaper accusing Year 8 student Alex of littering you must give her the chance to tell her side of the story, even if there is proof that she littered.

Independence

The MEAA ethics code states that journalists can't allow their personal interests or beliefs to affect their stories. It also says they can't let gifts influence their work.

If you were reporting that a fictional Choco Rocko Milk factory was closing, you couldn't let your personal feelings affect how you wrote the story. You shouldn't say: 'It's a very sad day because I can't buy the best chocolate milk in the country anymore.'

Or: 'It's great news that Choco Rocko Milk factory is closing. It made horrible chocolate milk that gave me a sore stomach.'

And if Choco Rocko Milk sent free chocolate milk to your student radio station you couldn't let that affect your story about the company either. It would be even better to tell your audience you'd received it.

Being responsible

Owning up to your mistakes is another part of being an honest reporter. If you get something wrong, you should correct the mistake and let the audience know.

It might look something like this.

> **CORRECTION**
> In the article, 'Circus life' published Saturday May 7, we incorrectly said Mo Mo was a clown. Mo Mo is an acrobat.
>
> We apologise for the mistake.

Setting your own rules

If you decide to start your own newspaper or program, think about the rules that should guide you and your fellow reporters now and in the future. Begin by writing down why the news outlet exists, who it's for, what you'll cover and how you'll deal with problems when they arise.

That's what they did at *The Spectator*.

The Spectator

The Stuyvesant High School Newspaper

"The Pulse of the Student Body"

Volume 110 No. 11   March 13, 2020   stuyspec.com

Turn to pages 11-22 for SING! Coverage

Stuyvesant's Science Olympiad Team Wins Regional Competition

By MAX KOSTER, DERRICK LIN, CHRISTOPHER SULLIVAN, and JAMES LEE

Nerves of Stuyvesant competitors from the Science Olympiad (SciOly) team were jangly as Townsend Harris High School jumped to an early lead at the NYC Science Olympiad Regionals. Schools across the city came to Grover Cleveland High School on February 8 to compete. Despite early anxiety, Stuyvesant swept subsequent parts of the competition and took home their third consecutive regional victory.

While SciOly members were confident in their abilities, they were up against strong opponents at Regionals. "We knew we were one of the top three schools going in, with Townsend Harris and Staten Island Tech being our biggest competitors, but we never 100 percent expected to win. The award ceremony, when each specific competition's winner is declared, occurs at the end of the tournament, so no one

knows who the winner is until then. This built up a lot of suspense, ultimately making the victory more worthwhile," said junior Daniel Gordon, who is on the chemistry team.

Not only did SciOly win,

but they also set a record for the lowest points at the NYC Regionals with 90 points. Points are awarded in the competition based on placement, with first place receiving one point, second receiving two points, and so forth. The team

with the least amount of points wins the overall competition. SciOly uses the meticulous and experimental nature of science to compete. Events are split into two divisions, Tech and Study, both

of which participated in the recent regional competition. The Tech division is the hands-on aspect of SciOly that creates projects that cor-

continued on page 2

Stuyvesant Hosts Annual Black History Month Dinner

By STEPHY CHEN, JENNY LIU, MADELYN MAO, and VEDAANT SHAH

"[Though] I do like to highlight the struggles that our predecessors have gone through to allow us to enjoy these things, just the celebration of it makes it more meaningful [...] a celebration both acknowledges the struggles and celebrates the future," junior and Black Students League (BSL) Vice President Tolulope Lawal said. The annual Black History Month dinner was hosted on February 27, which consisted of a StuyFlow performance and recitations of poems by Lawal and former Stuyvesant student and dropout from '06 to '09 Alexis Wint.

The event was coordinated by BSL, which aims to spread awareness of black culture, and ASPIRA, which aims to promote the empowerment of Hispanic and

Latino communities. Both clubs are part of StuyUnity, a larger coalition founded by SPARK advisor Angel Colon.

The opening remarks of the dinner were made by members of both BSL and ASPIRA, including co-Presidents senior Gordon Ebanks and junior Falina Ognus and Vice Presidents junior Sarai Pridgen and Tolulope Lawal. They introduced themselves and spoke on the significance of Black History month, which is celebrated every February. Colon and Principal Eric Contreras continued by explaining the importance of celebrating and spreading awareness of different cultures within the Stuyvesant community.

The StuyFlow performances, which had not been included in past dinners, followed and helped convey the themes of the dinner and the collaboration between BSL and AS-

continued on page 2

FEATURES

Coronavirus: Stuyvesant Students Share Their Thoughts

Features writers investigate both how Stuyvesant students are directly responding to COVID-19 and to the rising anti-Asian sentiment across New York City.

SEE PAGE 6

OPINIONS

Don't Spark It

Opinions writer Aaron Visser describes the value of literature and encourages the Stuyvesant community to complete their assigned reading rather than skim plot summaries.

SEE PAGE 9

Talia Kahan

Erin Lee

The Spectator's charter

The Spectator is the student newspaper at Stuyvesant High School in the USA, and it has an official charter which sets out the rules for how the paper is run.

The students working on the paper change often, so it's useful to have guidelines about what can and cannot be printed.

Students Erin Lee and Talia Kahan shared the role of editor-in-chief at the paper for one year, but *The Spectator* was first published more than a century ago in 1915!

Erin and Talia say the charter matters for two reasons.

'First, we reference the charter when making editorial decisions and changes,' they said. 'Second, we feel that it is important for the charter to be publicly available because we want our readership to know how we operate and what rules we set for ourselves.'

'Having our charter accessible online automatically holds us accountable for our actions and ensures that we are not, purposefully or otherwise, violating our own rules.'

The charter came in handy during school production time. The newspaper's entertainment reporter planned to write a review of a school stage musical called *SING!*. But the journalist also helped write the play's script. Was it fair for someone so heavily involved in the musical to also decide whether it was good or not? The charter said no.

'We consulted the charter and it confirmed that members of *SING!* could not write reviews,' Erin and Talia said.

Breaking it down

The Spectator's charter has four sections. These explain why the paper exists and how it's run, describe the roles of staff and detail how to deal with corrections. They also set out how reporters can remain fair and balanced.

Following is the Statement of Purpose, the first section of *The Spectator*'s charter. You can use this to inspire the guidelines for your own newsroom.

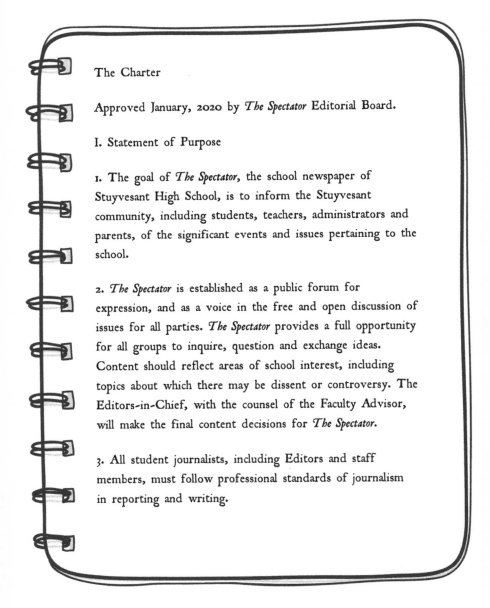

The Charter

Approved January, 2020 by *The Spectator* Editorial Board.

I. Statement of Purpose

1. The goal of *The Spectator*, the school newspaper of Stuyvesant High School, is to inform the Stuyvesant community, including students, teachers, administrators and parents, of the significant events and issues pertaining to the school.

2. *The Spectator* is established as a public forum for expression, and as a voice in the free and open discussion of issues for all parties. *The Spectator* provides a full opportunity for all groups to inquire, question and exchange ideas. Content should reflect areas of school interest, including topics about which there may be dissent or controversy. The Editors-in-Chief, with the counsel of the Faculty Advisor, will make the final content decisions for *The Spectator*.

3. All student journalists, including Editors and staff members, must follow professional standards of journalism in reporting and writing.

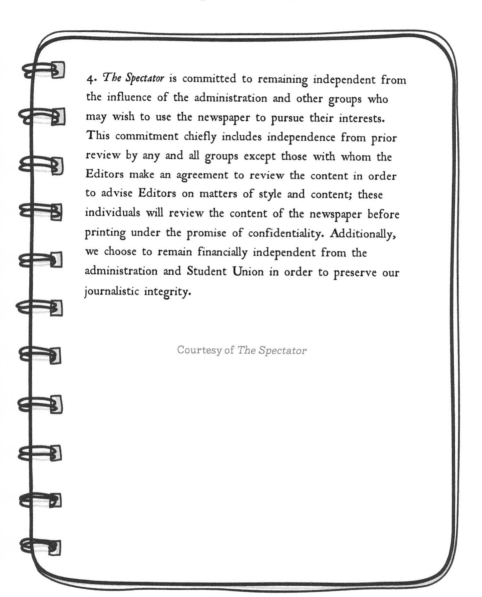

4. *The Spectator* is committed to remaining independent from the influence of the administration and other groups who may wish to use the newspaper to pursue their interests. This commitment chiefly includes independence from prior review by any and all groups except those with whom the Editors make an agreement to review the content in order to advise Editors on matters of style and content; these individuals will review the content of the newspaper before printing under the promise of confidentiality. Additionally, we choose to remain financially independent from the administration and Student Union in order to preserve our journalistic integrity.

Courtesy of *The Spectator*

PART IV

GET READY TO PUBLISH

16

BEING A CLEVER CREATOR

The next step on your journalism journey is to become a skilled publisher or broadcaster.

You might be a publisher already and not have realised. When you post something on the internet, you are a creator. It could be a photo, a piece of writing, a video, a comment or audio recording. Once you put it out there for others to look at, read, watch or hear, you have published your work.

That's a big responsibility. And it's one you want to take seriously.

You need to understand what you are saying, why you're saying it and what impact it might have on others.

When you publish, you create a permanent record of your stories. At that point, you no longer have control over what happens to them. Your work might be copied and shared. People could comment on it. Some may like it, others may not.

Being aware of this will make you a more careful, considered journalist and publisher.

Be respectful

As you consider how to set up your school newsroom or produce your first newspaper, remember the important critical thinking skills that already make you a great reporter.

Be clear about your own point of view and how it might differ from your fellow reporters and people in your audience. Consider how others might feel. You can never please everyone. But you can be fair and respectful.

Be realistic

Don't put too much pressure on yourself. Don't try to create a 40-page weekly student newspaper on your own! Take it one step at a time. First, gather your ideas and the support you need.

A news publisher has to be organised to be successful. Think about what you need before you begin.

Consider:

- time
- support from peers
- support from trusted adults
- equipment and tools
- funding.

Why publish?

Understand why you want to become a publisher. Is it for fun, to inform, create a community, help your career or to learn something new? Maybe it's for an assignment or because you love to write.

Appreciating why will help you plan and create your news service. It takes time to produce a story and more time again to put together a program or publication. Knowing what motivates you will help carry you through the challenging times.

What to publish?

There are lots of different kinds of news and special interest publications. If you love sport, your news outlet might only cover that. Someone passionate about the arts could review plays and exhibitions. General news includes all the random, exciting, new and important things happening in your community, across the country and around the world. Newspapers and TV bulletins tend to cover all these stories.

You can be creative too. You could sing the news or use poetry to keep your audience informed.

A TV show in Africa's Uganda, *NewzBeat*, proves you can be creative when presenting news stories. The show featured hip-hop artists as journalists – called 'raporters' and 'newsicians' – rapping the news.

The five-minute news program covered everything from Uganda's harsh laws to politics in the Ukraine and west Africa's Ebola outbreak. One young presenter even rapped about plastic bag bans: 'Major supermarket chains have shared more good news. From now on recyclable paper is the only bag they will use.'

How to publish

Having a clear plan about how to publish or broadcast will help in the long run. You need to be practical, consider what you're good at, what you like, and what's possible with the resources available. Ask yourself some questions.

RIGHT There was a news story about Uganda's *NewzBeat* TV show in the Australian newspaper, *Crinkling News*.

Rap, rap, rapping the news

By **Amy Fallon**

IN A COUNTRY where journalists who report the news can get into trouble from the government, hip-hop artists turned journalists - "raporters" and "newsicians" as they're called - are rapping the news and pushing the boundaries.

In Uganda, as in many other countries around the world, topics such as politics, corruption and land rights are considered off-limits by the government.

There have been 26 arrests, physical attacks and threats to journalists in Uganda this year, says the African Freedom of Expression Exchange, which is a network of press freedom organisations.

And another African country, Eritrea, was ranked as the most censored in the world last year, says the Committee to Protect Journalists. Ethiopia came fourth.

But a popular TV show in Uganda, *NewzBeat*, covers everything from Uganda's harsh laws to the political situation in Ukraine to West Africa's Ebola epidemic.

It's a brave thing to do because before the east African country's elections in March the government detained journalists, blocked social media and banned stories about protests.

NEWS WITH 'RHYME AND REASON'

One of the presenters is 15-year-old rapper Zoe Kabuye, also known as MC Loy, who has rapped on Uganda's high youth unemployment:

"Even with a degree or diploma"

"Finding work is still a drama."

And on the country's plastic bag ban:

"Major supermarket chains have shared more good news"

"From now on recyclable paper is the only bag they will use."

More recently, she covered a story about a cancer crisis in Uganda:

NewzBeat presenters Zoe Kabuye, also known as MC Loy, Sharon Bwogi, also known as Lady Slyke, and her daughter, Zion Sheebah, in the show's Kampala studio.
PHOTO **Amy Fallon**

"Earlier this year the cancer institute's only radiotherapy machine broke down"

"Beyond repair leaving many cancer patients across the country in despair."

KIDS ARE TUNING IN

Before *NewzBeat* many children had no interest in news and current affairs.

"Some youth never used to watch news – they hated it and used to say it's boring." says MC Loy, who is still in school but also raps in public places in her spare time.

"But many people on Facebook are like 'What time is *NewzBeat* on?' "

Uganda's youngest "newsician", nine-year-old Zion Sheebah, recently joined the program as its youth reporter.

Zion – the daughter of Ugandan rappers Sharon Bwogi, known as Lady Slyke, and Daniel Kisekka, known as DJ Nesta, who are also *NewzBeat* presenters – says children's rights is her favourite subject to rap about.

NewzBeat is screened in both English and Uganda's local language, Luganda, on channel NTV every Saturday and Sunday. It runs for five minutes and has local, regional and international stories. About 160,000 people watch every episode.

It is now also screening in Tanzania, and hopes to expand to other African countries.

South African students from Chief Albert Luthuli Primary and High School in Daveyton on June 15 in Johannesburg to mark the 40th anniversary of the 1976 uprising in Soweto against apartheid. PHOTO **Mujahid Safodien/AFP**

Around the world – Venice

By **Dallas Kilponen**

Here I have captured some kids playing chase around a fountain in the courtyard of the Doge's Palace in St Mark's Square in Venice.

It is a tourist highlight, with its incredible architecture, grand rooms and ornate artworks. The palace was built between 1172 and 1178 but two huge fires,

the first in 1483 and the next in 1547 destroyed most of the original building.

In 1797 the palace was ruled by the French after Napoleon occupied Italy but was returned to the people of Italy in 1866.

A gondolier on the Grand Canal in Venice at dusk. PHOTOS **Dallas Kilponen**

- Will I create and publish on my own? Do I want to be part of a news team or club? Can my school, friends or family help run my news service?
- Do I want to write, record audio, film, photograph, draw or edit?
- Will I produce a newspaper, podcast, videos, vlog, blog or photography? Which kind of media would suit me best?
- What's my age? There are age guidelines for using certain social media platforms. Do I need a trusted adult to advise me?
- Do I need permission from the principal to publish on a school platform?
- Who is the audience? Where do they usually get their news? They need to be able to access your stories. There's not much point choosing a social media platform, such as Facebook, YouTube or Instagram, if your audience can't access it because they're too young.

You might broadcast a podcast on your school website as well as on a hosting platform. You could print a student newspaper or create an electronic version and have a supervising teacher email it to your classmates, parents and staff. Depending on your age, you might want to create your own blog or vlog and post it directly on a social media platform.

Responsibility

Becoming a news publisher or broadcaster is a big responsibility. You are in charge of the information shared with your audience and the public. You should be able to defend your work and stand by it. Your audience will need a way to contact you and your outlet. Think through this carefully and find a trusted adult to help you decide how you and your fellow reporters communicate with the public.

Contributing to public conversations and information is important and so is your voice. It's a great opportunity to show that you've worked hard to create honest and accurate pieces of work.

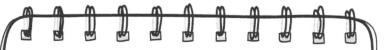

Privacy

If you want to include anyone aged under 18 in your news stories you should get permission from their parents, guardians or teachers.
You also need to be mindful of their privacy.
If you plan to publish your stories online and make them accessible to the general public, you can choose to publish only the first names of students — especially if you include other identifying information such as school names, suburbs and classes.

17

START YOUR OWN
NEWSPAPER

Now you know how to be a reporter and you've thought through the steps to becoming a publisher. You believe in people's right to know what's going on around them and the importance of sharing the stories that help build a community.

It's time to start your very own newspaper!

You'll need staff, including editors, reporters, photographers and artists. You'll have to think about who will design the newspaper and carefully place the stories and images on each page so everyone can easily read them. What about printing or publishing, and what if this costs money? How often will you publish? The paper needs to be shared with your audience – distributed – and you'll need at least one trusted adult, such as a teacher or parent, to help.

Take a look at some newspapers produced for adults before you get stuck into planning your own. Notice how stories are ordered on each page, the different sections, what subjects are covered, how the pages are numbered and the edition date.

What's in a newspaper?

Front page

Puff: Image and/or words pointing to a story inside the newspaper

Date and price: The date the edition was published, the edition number and a price if there is one

Masthead: Title of the newspaper

Splash: Main, or lead, story on the front page

Headline: Title of the news story

Byline: Author of the story or person who took the photo

To be continued: If the story goes onto another page inside the newspaper, tell your readers which page

Graphic: A drawing, normally done on a computer, like a map or graph

Caption: Description of an image or graphic

Page two

Picture byline: A photo or image of the author

Note from the editor: You might want to say hello to your readers and tell them about what's in each issue

Index: Page numbers and descriptions showing your readers where to find selected stories or sections

Contact details: The main people responsible for making the newspaper and how to contact them

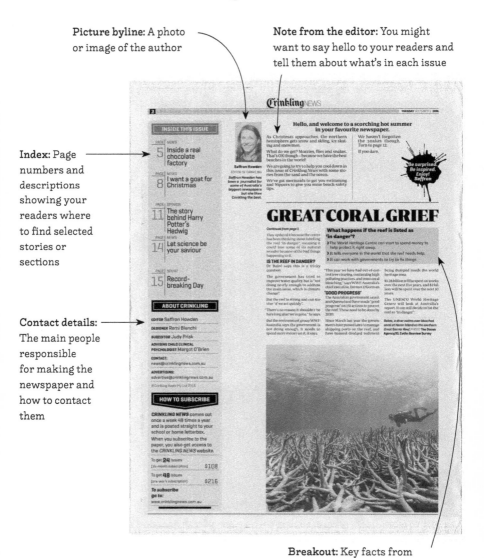

Breakout: Key facts from the story made to stand out

Puzzles and games

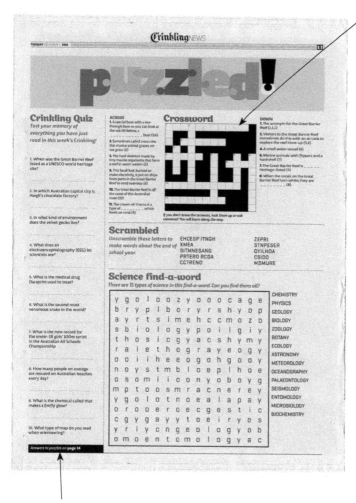

You might want to consider a puzzles page in your newspaper, including a quiz, crossword, word search or anagrams where readers have to put the letters in the right order to form a word.

Sudoku, mazes and word wheels are other ideas.

Having competitions with prizes is also a great way to get new readers and involve more people in your newspaper.

You'll have to put the answers on another page of the paper so your readers can check them!

157

Sections

Clearly labelled sections are a nice way for readers to make their way through your newspaper.

You might have a page just for opinions, a section for sport, science or one for reviews of books, movies and video games.

There are plenty of things to consider before you can publish your first front page. But let's brainstorm the fun stuff. Use the following guide to help plan your school newspaper.

Title

The name of a newspaper is sometimes called a 'masthead'. You might want to use a particular font, so the title looks the same for every edition. Or design a special title by drawing it.

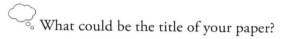 What could be the title of your paper?

Colours and font

Having a colour scheme and consistent font helps people recognise the newspaper. You could use different colours for each section to help your readers tell the difference.

 Colours

Pages

Each edition could be the same number of pages to help with planning how many stories to cover. Each page might have two or three stories on it, including pictures or illustrations.

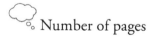 Number of pages

---

Staff

Editor/s, designers, reporters, photographers, artists, subeditors, supervising editor (adult) – your newspaper will need lots of staff to share the work around. You might want help from someone with design skills to make sure everything looks neat on the pages.

If you've forgotten what each staff member does, go back to Chapter 10, page 89 where we created an example newsroom.

 Jobs

Timetable

You may want to publish your newspaper once a term, every two terms or even once a year. Think about the work involved and how much time everyone has to spend on it.

 Publication dates

---

Sections

What kinds of stories will your newspaper cover? Some examples are news and events, sport, environment, science, technology, music and art, puzzles and opinions. Will you have cartoons or comics in each edition? And book or movie reviews?

 Topics

Equipment

Ask for adult assistance with this. You might need a camera, a sound recorder or dictaphone for interviews, notepads and pens. You'll need access to a computer and maybe even design software.

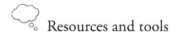 Resources and tools

---

Publishing

Distributing your newspaper to students or the school community is key. If you're going to print each edition, you'll have to work with a trusted adult to either raise money for printing or get the school or parents to print it. If it's sent to the readers by email, someone from the school will need to organise this.

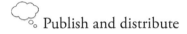 Publish and distribute

---

Contact

You may need to set up a special email address or make a 'submissions' box at school so people can send you story ideas or submit reviews.

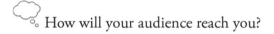 How will your audience reach you?

Once you've decided on the essentials you could consider writing a 'code of ethics' for your publication, a set of basic rules everyone who works for the newspaper has to follow. This might include being kind, fair and honest in all your stories and the way you go about gathering information to write them.

Having a trusted adult on board from the start is very important. They can help you research printing and publishing, assist in raising money if needed, publicise the paper so everyone knows about it and maybe do a final check of each edition before it's distributed to the school community.

Creating and publishing a newspaper is a big responsibility. But the first time you see your name in print as the author of a story – your byline – is pretty exciting. The hard work is worth it!

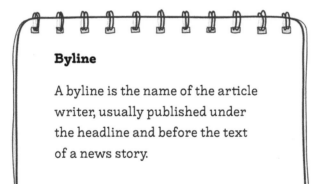

Byline

A byline is the name of the article writer, usually published under the headline and before the text of a news story.

18

MINI MEDIA MOGULS

You're never too young to start your own media empire. Well, maybe not an empire. But in Australia and around the world, there are plenty of examples of students producing newspapers for their classmates and local communities.

Some schools also run journalism, news or media clubs as a way to encourage students to get involved and help share, plan and create something unique.

The Once In A Lifetime News

Publishing a newspaper on a regular basis is fun, but it's also a lot of hard work. Producing one issue as a class project is a good way to start. And that's exactly what the students did at Katoomba Public School in the Blue Mountains west of Sydney.

The Once In A Lifetime News was put together over one term by the combined Year 2 and 3 class with teacher Steve Gero. 'When I raised the idea, we could make our own newspaper there was a lot of excitement,' Mr Gero said.

Mini media moguls storm the news

BY **Heather Zubek**

THE team at *Crinkling News* should be afraid. Very afraid. Kids are producing their own newspapers, and they are really good.

They're also learning about media literacy, deadlines, how news is reported and the importance of checking facts.

"I've learnt that you need a very good balance of serious and funny stories," says Noah, who's 11, from Trinity Grammar School in Melbourne.

"If you have too much serious stuff, no one will read it."

UNDERSTANDING THE NEWS

Trinity Times comes out monthly and sells for $1. The money goes to a charity and the boys raised $113 for the Cancer Council of Australia from their first issue.

Up to 15 boys spend lunchtimes working on stories that include school and sporting news, fun facts and comics.

Jimmy, also 11, believes everyone should be able to understand the news.

"Preps to older kids read our paper so it's important that I try to explain difficult words when I'm writing articles," he says.

A RAT'S TALE

A brother and sister from the Victorian town of Ballarat are taking their first steps towards a media career.

Audrey, 10, and George, seven, attended the junior journalist workshop in Melbourne in 2016 that was run by the editor of *Crinkling News*, Saffron Howden.

"I learnt how to write articles and a good first sentence," says Audrey.

"It also gave me the idea to start our own newspaper, *The Monthly Rat*."

With friends Noah and Emily they have put together eight issues.

"I'm the sports reporter and bit of an editor," says George. "I'm not the best editor yet as I don't know how to read everything."

Each month there are 300 copies printed. Stories include what's happening in the lives of the writers, and reviews of books and local cafes.

OUT OF THE BLUE

Ms Howden also visited students at Lindfield East Public School in Sydney in June to discuss writing for newspapers. Now Year 6 is ready to publish the first issue of *The Blue Lyrebird*.

"We called it that because our school's crest is a lyrebird and our school uniform is blue," says Maddie, who's 11.

The Blue Lyrebird has school happenings, recipes, environmental news, interviews and advice on problems in the playground.

"It took a lot of commitment from everyone to put this together but it's hard getting ideas for interviews," says Aryana, who's 12.

"Once kids read our newspaper they will be more engaged as the articles relate to them," says Georgia, 11.

HOT CHIPS SET TO SIZZLE

"Our school is called Camp Hill Primary School and we call ourselves CHIPS, so we thought the newspaper should be called *Hot Chips News*," says the chief editor, Matisse, 11, from Brisbane.

So far two issues have been published, each with 200 copies.

"We have articles about people like conservationist Jane Goodall, a "Meet the Author" section and writers like Elliott who gives fishing tips," says Matisse.

"Working on a newspaper helps me read more and it also helps me find friends who are interested in the same things as me."

This story was made possible by funding from the Copyright Agency's cultural fund.

The Monthly Rat, issue eight.

HOT CHIPS NEWS

Hot Chips News, second issue.

What is media literacy?

> It's the ability to think about the things we see or hear in the media – whether it's online, in newspapers or on TV – and be able to know what messages are being sent and why.

> Somebody who is media literate can tell the difference between paid advertising and news, and between opinion and fact. They can also create media.

SOURCE **Common Sense Media.**

Top, founder of Trinity Times, Noah, 11, with the first edition and, above, the editorial team working on the Trinity Times.
PHOTOS **Elizabeth Clancy**

Meet Claire, our fourth junior editor

"TO be, or not to be." That is the question the 16th century English playwright William Shakespeare first asked, and it is the question Claire Oh continues to ponder.

Claire, who's nine and lives in Sydney, is the fourth junior assistant editor to join the *Crinkling News* team.

She's a massive fan of poetry, especially the works of the Bard.

"Ever since I read one of William Shakespeare's poems [I was hooked]," she says. "Poetry can be short, but [it] expresses much more than a story."

MURDER, MAGIC AND MYSTERY

Claire loves Shakespeare's stories because they combine life and death, love and revenge, grief and jealousy with a fair portion of murder, magic and mystery, just like the Harry Potter series, which is Claire's other favourite thing to read.

"My favourite author is JK Rowling, because she created a world that everyone could enter [with] her magical books," she says.

TO TEACH, OR TO DIRECT?

With such a love of literature, it's no surprise Claire's favourite thing to do at school is writing.

She says being a part of the *Crinkling News* team will help her hone her writing skills even more, and help her decide between her two dream jobs.

"I want to be a teacher because I want to help encourage students to give everything a go, and to take risks," she says.

"[But I also] want to be a [movie] director because I can work behind the scenes to create a masterpiece other people can enjoy."

CARING FOR THE WORLD

There's one thing Claire loves more than reading, and that's the environment.

"I wish people knew how much pollution there really is in the world," she says.

"People are cutting down the amount of natural environment that are habitats for animals [and whenever] a tree is cut down, it releases greenhouse gases like carbon dioxide [that's] causing global warming."

ABOVE IT ALL

If she had a superpower, Claire would want to be able to fly high above the forests and trees.

"My superpower would be to fly, because I would feel free to soar like a bird. My nemesis would be anyone who hates reading," she says.

As Shakespeare advised, so Claire lives: "This above all: to thine own self be true."

INSIDE:
Ronaldo Vs Messi
Who is better?
SPORT, page 12

Bigger than a T-Rex?
NATURE, page 6

The
Once In A Lifetime News

A newspaper for kids by kids

SCHOOL'S OUT

2/3G students try out the seating in the new outdoor learning area.

By **Dominic Newling and Sebastian Salter**

IT HAS NO WALLS. IT HAS NO ROOF. WHAT IS IT? THE OUTDOOR LEARNING CENTRE!

Katoomba Public School is very excited that there is a new outdoor spot for kids to use. The outdoor centre is a special place for connecting to Country, it is also special for our Koori Club people and for the whole school to come out and enjoy nature and help create this area. It is such a special place in our school and it is going to become even more special over the next few years as plants grow. It is going to be used so classes can come out and sit in a circle and do circle time activities, and it is also going to be a place where *continued page 3*

HELPING THE HOMELESS

By **Lily Redd And Bella Williamson**

DO YOU WANT TO LEARN ABOUT HOMELESS PEOPLE? WELL THIS IS YOUR ARTICLE.

On the 9th of November 2/3G had a visit from Rosa from Earth Recovery. Earth Recovery is an organisation in Katoomba that helps homeless people.

We invited Rosa because 2/3G is reading a book by David Walliams about a homeless man called Mr Stink, so we were interested in homeless people after a while.

Continued page 3

Katoomba Public School in NSW published a
one-off newspaper edition as a class project.

166

To begin with, the class brainstormed ideas and settled on five main sections: news and events, interviews, science, environment and sport. They also included comics and puzzles. They selected two student editors and section editors. Each article had to have a great headline and first sentence to capture the readers' attention.

There was a competition to name the newspaper and the students responsible for the top three ideas gave a speech to the rest of the class to convince everyone theirs was the best.

In the end, the whole school became involved and raised money for the paper to be printed at a real newspaper printing press. Some parents bought space in the paper to advertise their businesses. The Year 2 and 3 students organised a vegetarian nachos day and mufti day and ran a homemade lemonade stall to get donations.

'It was a real push to get it done. The whole school was really excited,' Mr Gero said. Once the paper was printed each copy was sold for $1. They raised so much money they had $500 left over to donate to the local homeless charity.

Blackburn Lake Times

Not every student journalist will have a teacher like Mr Gero to help them set up a newsroom. Luke Eaton had been writing news stories and reviews for a couple of years for local and national newspapers when, in Year 6,

LukeEaton

he decided to start his own at Blackburn Lake Primary School in Melbourne, Victoria.

Luke made a prototype, or sample, of a newspaper to show his school it could be done. He asked a friend's mum who worked as a graphic designer – someone who puts text and images together for magazines, newspapers and advertisements – to teach him how to use the computer software needed to design the paper.

After setting up an email address for people to contact him, he made speeches at school assembly and in individual classes asking students to submit articles for publication. He also got his friends to help out.

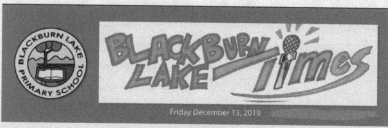

Friday December 13, 2019

First Edition of Blackburn Lake Times

Welcome readers to the very first edition of the Blackburn Lake Times! There are some great articles and interviews that have been submitted. We hope that you enjoy reading the first edition of this unique new newspaper.

New Logo at the Times

According to sources inside this great primary school, it was time for a new logo for the newspaper. A competition was run, and there were no limits to the imagination of the entries submitted. The winning entry, by   of grade 4, can now be proudly seen in the Blackburn Lake Times. Well done to all of the amazing entries.

Blackburn Lake Celebrity-Stumpy

In case you didn't know, Stumpy is the local area celebrity on Lake Road on the boundary of Blackburn Lake Sanctuary. Stumpy shared some amazing insights as to who he was with me.

First I asked Stumpy "who created you?" "Well" said Stumpy "First I started off as a tree in Blackburn Lake, which grew over the fence. When my tree fell down, the local council cut it down, but left me there to look over the lake. I became a celebrity when my special friends started dressing me up in fabulous outfits! For the first few years it was just hats (my special friends wanted to make sure that I was sunsmart!) but since December last year my special friends have put me in more and more exciting outfits."

"How many costumes do you have Stumpy?"

"I have lots of costumes. I love dressing up and changing my look. I especially love celebrating holidays, and special events."

Being at the Lake, "what animals do you see at night?"

"I see lots of animals at night, lots of possums, owls and the occasional fox."

"Do birds get up close to you?"

"Yes birds do get up close to me- I think it's just because they are jealous of my outfits!"

"Do you have any friends?"

"I have lots of friends- everyone who comes to visit me each day is my friend! I also have lots of friends who are dogs- they like to stop by on their walks with their humans."

To keep up with all of Stumpy's outfits and friends, visit him

1

After lots of hard work and determination, the first edition of the *Blackburn Lake Times* was published! His parents printed copies for him to share at the Year 6 writers' festival. 'They loved it,' Luke said.

Before he left to go to high school, Luke wrote a set of instructions so students could continue to produce the *Times* even after he had gone.

Orange Street News

Young reporters don't have to work out of a classroom. Hilde Lysiak was eight years old when she decided to start a newspaper from her home in Pennsylvania in the United States of America. The monthly *Orange Street News* covered everything that affected her community – from local sporting heroes and suburb clean-ups to much harder news, such as drug busts and robberies.

'I don't remember a time when I didn't want to be a reporter,' Hilde said when she was 11. She even reported on a death! Lots of people criticised her and her parents for that story because they thought she was too young.

'What upset me was that they weren't criticising my reporting,' she said. 'They were criticising my age. And that I was a girl! I wanted them to know I was going to keep reporting the news.'

Hilde's tip for young reporters is, 'If you take yourself seriously, other people will take you seriously too.'

'If you stay focused on the story, finding the who, what, where, when, why and how, then you won't have time to be nervous!'

19

I'M A MULTIMEDIA REPORTER

Radio, television and video are great, accessible platforms to tell news. If this is the kind of journalism for you there are lots of possibilities. You could produce a podcast or a series of audio stories for a website. You might film the news and publish it on a social media platform.

Before you commit, you'll have to investigate the technology needed, such as computer software programs to record, edit and publish.

You'll also need to consider the age guidelines for the platforms you decide to use. Many social media platforms require users to be a minimum age of 12 or 13. This will affect you as a journalist as well as the audience you are trying to reach.

There's no point using most social media platforms if your audience is mainly primary school students as there are age limits that would stop many from accessing the content. You will need to find out what the age minimums are for any platforms you want to use and check with a trusted adult.

Elwood Primary presents
6T Kids' Podcast

A 6T Kids' Podcast logo drawn by Angus Penfold,
aged 11, who loves old-fashioned animations.

Unless you can convince a local community radio station to put your student show to air, the simplest way to publish an audio program is to create a podcast.

That is what Elwood Primary School in Melbourne did.

Year 6 teacher, Tim Ghys, helped his class set up a podcast as a way to share what was happening at the school with the wider community. And it's a student-driven program. 'We have three students run each episode and we rotate hosts to give everyone a turn,' Mr Ghys said. 'They decide what to do.'

For each 20-minute episode, the three hosts plan, interview, write and present the podcast. Mr Ghys said he trains other students to record, edit and design logos to involve as many students as possible.

'It's important to give students a voice and for them to connect with the community. And this podcast is another way to do that. We've had grandparents from around the world listening to the episodes,' he said.

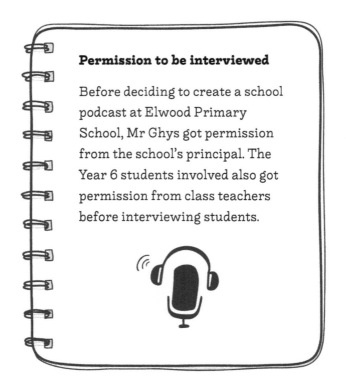

Permission to be interviewed

Before deciding to create a school podcast at Elwood Primary School, Mr Ghys got permission from the school's principal. The Year 6 students involved also got permission from class teachers before interviewing students.

If you're planning to set up a school podcast, here are Mr Ghys's tips.

- Equipment

  'At a minimum you need microphones, headphones and a computer. We use microphones, stands, microphone leads, headphones and an amplifier box that plugs into a computer. We had most of the equipment in the school's music room. We also occasionally use a dictaphone if we are recording interviews out in the yard.'

- Software

  'You'll need a music software program to record and edit the audio on a computer. I did some research and found a quality program that was safe, inexpensive and flexible to suit our needs.'

- Publishing

  'You need to set up an account with a podcast hosting platform that will store and distribute your audio files. We send each finished episode to the service and it puts our episodes on the main podcast directories, so people can find and listen to our podcasts. We also publish the podcasts on the school's website.'

Nellie Sturtevant

Q&A with student podcast host:
Nellie Sturtevant

Eleven-year-old Nellie Sturtevant is one of the hosts of
6T's podcast at Elwood Primary.

Why did you want to be involved in the podcast?
'I thought it would be fun and something I hadn't tried
before. Also, I felt I would regret not having a go.'

What has been your favourite bit?
'Interviewing people. Also recording is fun. One time
me and another girl in my class were interviewing
two other girls. We had so much fun and had to
re-record it so many times because we couldn't stop
laughing.'

What skills have you picked up?

'I'm more confident with speaking. Also developing questions and things to do in the podcast in a short amount of time.'

What have you included in your episodes?

'We put all sorts of things into the podcast. We did the Grade 5/6 choir. The episode I did we interviewed our principal. Sometimes there are jokes, announcements and stories.'

How does it feel to listen to something you created?

'Proud and a feeling of accomplishment. Sometimes you feel nervous that you sound terrible on the podcast and that it is out in the world. But at the end of the day you feel awesome that you did the podcast.'

TV-style news

It's more complicated to create a TV-style news program and you'll need more equipment. But you could share your work on the school website or a social media platform like YouTube or Instagram.

As with setting up a podcast, you need a trusted adult or teacher to help choose equipment, computer software programs and a suitable publishing platform.

And again you'll need to check any age minimums for social media platforms. If you're doing something at school, you'll need permission from your principal and help from a teacher or two.

Ararat College presents *AC News*

Jack Ward

Student journalist, Jack Ward

Just before Jack Ward was to enter Year 8, he had an idea: he wanted to create a TV-style news program at his school, Ararat College in country Victoria. He approached his English teacher, got some students together and, within a couple of months, *AC News* was born.

Initially stories were posted on Instagram. 'We wanted to use Instagram because a lot of our students, who we wanted to target first, were using that platform,' Jack said.

The team decided to produce short, TV-style news stories – where a host introduced or presented one story.

They covered a great deal in the first year, including a fire that destroyed a local primary school which Jack and many fellow students had attended. 'We were all in shock to begin with but we were on the scene that day, posting live stories and covering what was happening,' he said.

AC News soon evolved. After getting approval from parents and teachers, the news team launched a Facebook page and a dedicated news website. The audience grew from fellow students to include the wider community.

'We started producing at least six articles a week and had a team of about 20 students. The website grew massively,' Jack said. 'We were getting thousands of views on the website every month and we were still doing the TV-style segments.'

There was also a bit of healthy competition. Jack explained further:

'We have a local paper in Ararat and we tried to publish before that paper, which was great for us. We were working to deadlines. We got the story, we put it together and we put it out there, ensuring the quality was as good as it could be.

It was a huge learning experience. I mean, you're working in the real world. We were talking to people we would normally never speak to. You learn so many skills – not just writing and putting a bulletin together – but your people skills, your communication skills, and your work ethic.'

Jack stopped working on *AC News* in Year 10. The next year, he started his own community news podcast and began working at a local newspaper. And he did his schoolwork too, of course!

AC News supervising teacher, Lenny Sky

Secondary school teacher Lenny Sky worked with Jack on *AC News* and said setting up a news program helped all students involved.

'For students who may end up with a career in journalism it can really help develop their skills, contacts and experience,' she said. 'Others gain a range of media and teamwork skills. And some of our shy students really came out of their shells and developed confidence.'

Ms Sky said the website launch provided opportunities for those interested in photography, website management and writing. 'There were a number of students who loved writing reviews or reports, particularly avid gamers who just loved doing game reviews, while others wrote music and TV reviews,' she said.

A boom microphone is a microphone attached to an extendable arm.

Below are Ms Sky's tips for setting up TV-style news at school.

- Equipment
  'Initially we used a video camera, studio lights and a tripod from the [school] media department and a green screen to go behind the host. We used a computer software program for editing and an online tool to create our opening theme music. Over the years we updated our video cameras and expanded our equipment to include things like a boom microphone. We eventually purchased a teleprompter, which allowed students to read a script while looking directly into the camera. Before that we had kids holding up butcher's paper with scripts written in large font.'

What is a 'green screen'?
A green background used in filming which allows an image or background videoed separately to be added to the final footage viewers see.

- Budget
  'When we started, we were able to get away with using equipment already in the school. Once we wanted to improve operations – particularly for interviewing politicians and getting out into the community – applying for a grant from the school became invaluable. Jack wrote a grant request for the school council to approve and we had support from our school leadership.'

- Teacher involvement
  'In the first year I supervised meetings to help brainstorm ideas for stories, assign jobs and film. I was less involved in the second and third years as the students were older, more skilled and independent. Other staff members helped too, including the assistant principal who organised permissions for students to be off-site and drove them to film stories like the premier of Victoria opening a wind farm.'

- Three must-haves
  'Basic equipment, at least three committed students, and at least one media-savvy student or teacher.'

20

MAKING YOUR VOICE COUNT

Not everyone will want to start a media empire just yet. And setting up a newspaper or school news program is a big job. But you can still be involved in news and have a say in the big issues.

You could be a 'freelance' student reporter. As a freelance journalist you can write or produce stories for any media outlets. You aren't tied to just one. This might be specialist programs for young people, community media organisations or even major news outlets. Some news organisations will ask a freelance reporter to write just one story if the staff journalists don't have time.

Writing a letter to the editor of a newspaper is another way to get published. If you read a particular magazine and there is a story you would like to comment on, then get typing. Gather your facts, double-check them and compose your thoughts.

If you are really passionate about an issue or news story, you could write an opinion piece. Make sure you know who to send it to by looking up the name and contact details of the editor or producer so your work lands in the right person's inbox.

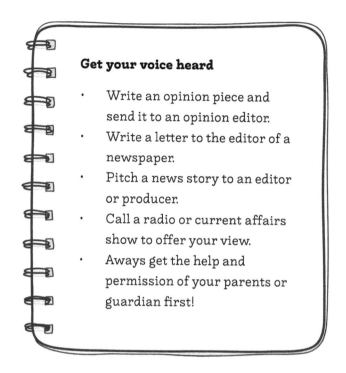

Get your voice heard

- Write an opinion piece and send it to an opinion editor.
- Write a letter to the editor of a newspaper.
- Pitch a news story to an editor or producer.
- Call a radio or current affairs show to offer your view.
- Aways get the help and permission of your parents or guardian first!

You can also write or produce a story and pitch it – try to convince an editor your idea is great, and they should publish it. You need to be very clear about what your story is, why it should be published, and be able to summarise all the interesting parts. Your ideas won't always be accepted. But you should always be respectful and gracious regardless of the outcome.

There are many publications and programs in Australia, and around the world, produced just for young people. It's worth checking if they have junior reporter programs or other initiatives to involve their audience.

Don't worry if your first story, letter or opinion piece doesn't get published. Learn from these experiences and keep trying.

This is also true if you try to set up a news program and it doesn't get off the ground. Or if your project only lasts a few months, a term or a year – that's okay too. You learn no matter how long your project runs. It's all experience.

The important thing is to make a start and try. Be creative and be yourself. Use your skills, passion and interests to inspire your ideas. Think about your audience and do lots of investigating! Be bold and try new ways of presenting.

Being a young reporter is an opportunity to use your voice. It's an exciting chance to use it in a way that not only informs people, but also helps make connections in your community.

Solli Raphael

Solli Raphael is a poet, author, activist and performer. Winner of the Australian Poetry Slam in 2017, he's written two published books called *Limelight* and *Spotlight*. Solli says young people's views are just as important as the opinions of adults.

'It is so important that young people not only have their voices heard, but have their voices acknowledged and accepted by those in power and in the media,' he said.

Solli Raphael

'When I was 12 and I first began speaking publicly about issues such as climate change, bullying, and environmental sustainability, having my thoughts and ideas heard made me feel that I was as valuable as any adult to my community.

For me, using my voice through my poetry, performances and books enables me to be an active part of the world and speak about issues that will affect my generation's future.'

Young people can have an important and positive impact on public discussions that affect their lives and the future. 'Every day more and more young people find their voice and stand up for what they believe in and stand up for our future,' Solli said.

'Today, the next young person to stand up for what they believe in could be you.'

Now it's time to make *your* voice count. We can't wait to see your stories!

RESOURCES

Offline

Notley, T, Dezuanni, M, Zhong, HF & Howden S,
'News and Australian Children: How Young
People Access, Perceive and are Affected by the
News', Research Report, Sydney, Western Sydney
University, Queensland University of Technology
and *Crinkling News*, 2017.

Raphael, S, *Limelight*, Puffin, Melbourne, 2018.

Raphael, S, *Spotlight*, Puffin, Melbourne, 2020.

Stephens, M, *A History of News*, Oxford University
Press, New York, 3rd edn, 2007.

Schudson, M, *Why Journalism Still Matters*, Polity
Press, Oxford, 2018.

Online

Alannah & Madeline Foundation, <amf.org.au>.

Australia's eSafety Commissioner, <esafety.gov.au>.

Behind the News, <abc.net.au/btn>.

Civic Online Reasoning, <cor.stanford.edu>.

Common Sense Media, <commonsensemedia.org>.

MEAA Journalist Code of Ethics, <meaa.org/meaa-media/code-of-ethics>.

MediaWise, <poynter.org/mediawise>.

RMIT ABC Fact Check, <abc.net.au/news/factcheck>.

The Spectator's charter, <stuyspec.com/about/our-charter>.

ACKNOWLEDGMENTS

Thanks to all the wonderful young reporters and journalism professionals who shared their experience and knowledge with us so we could share it with you in *Kid Reporter*. Thanks also for letting us reproduce your work and turn your photographs into fabulous illustrations.

Special mention to our agent Benython Oldfield, Judy Prisk for reading our manuscript, and everyone at NewSouth, including Elspeth Menzies, Paul O'Beirne and Josephine Pajor-Markus for helping bring this book to life.

We are forever grateful to all the readers, contributors and supporters of *Crinkling News*. Without the newspaper there would be no book.

From Saffron

Journalism is a team effort. Over 20 years in the industry so many talented people have helped me along the way. I'd like to especially acknowledge *Crinkling News* co-founder and designer Rémi Bianchi and my family members Jocelyn, Kristin and Erland Howden for volunteering behind the scenes. Thanks to Peter Fray, the peerless Judy Prisk (again!) Emma Horn, Lidia Valenzuela, Paula Pond, Margot O'Brien, Rebecca Bignell,

David Mallard, Grace Gregson and Diya Mehta. Collectively, these people made the newspaper possible.

I owe a debt of gratitude to JC and Tony Gillies for giving me my break as a cadet reporter at Australian Associated Press (AAP) and to the mastheads I have worked for, *The Sydney Morning Herald*, *The Daily Telegraph* and *The Northern Star*.

Finally, big hugs to my family and friends for their support over the years and through the writing of this book, especially my mum, dad and my husband and best friend, Rémi.

From Dhana

Thank you to all who encouraged me during my journalism career beginning with those at community radio stations, country newsrooms and local papers who helped me gain valuable work experience when starting out.

Thanks to the editors, producers and colleagues I worked with at *The Age* and the ABC's Melbourne and Sydney newsrooms – it was fabulous to work alongside so many talented professionals. To the team at *Behind the News*, thanks for giving me the privilege of presenting to a school-aged audience.

And a huge cheers to my immediate and extended family for their ongoing love and support – special mention to my parents Rody and Peter and my husband Adam.

INDEX

Lightning Source UK Ltd.
Milton Keynes UK
UKHW011412030321
379713UK00002B/605